D1271825

BEHAVIORALISM IN
POLITICAL SCIENCE

The Editor

HEINZ EULAU is Professor of Political Science at Stanford University and a member of the Stanford Institute of Political Studies. He received his B.A., M.A., and Ph.D. from the University of California at Berkeley. Professor Eulau has been an analyst in the Special War Policies Unit of the United States Department of Justice and an assistant editor of *The New Republic*. He has taught at Antioch College and was Visiting Legislative Research Professor at the University of California at Berkeley in 1961-62 and Visiting Professor at the Institute for Advanced Studies in Vienna in 1964-65. At present Professor Eulau is chairman of the Council of the Inter-University Consortium for Political Research and chairman of the Political Science Panel of the Behavioral and Social Sciences Survey Committee. He is the author of *Class and Party in the Eisenhower Years, The Behavioral Persuasion in Politics,* and *Journeys in Politics.* He has co-authored *The Legislative System* and *Lawyers in Politics,* and has edited or co-edited several other books, including *Political Behavior, Legislative Behavior,* and *Political Behavior in America.* He also contributes frequently to academic and professional symposia and journals.

BEHAVIORALISM

EDITED BY

IN POLITICAL
SCIENCE

Heinz Eulau
STANFORD UNIVERSITY

ATHERTON PRESS

New York 1969

Preface

This volume is one in a continuing series of
attempts to communicate to the student a feeling for what
behavioralism in the study of politics is all about—in this
case by presenting the polemical context in which the behavioral persuasion originated, grew, and matured.

In a first little book, published some years ago,[1] I tried to
set forth, in a simple manner unencumbered by references to
empirical research, what I thought the behavioral approaches
in political science were. Curiously, what I had thought was
the book's virtue was promptly criticized as its vice by my
good friend and fellow traveler in the political behavior
movement, Robert E. Lane. It seemed to Lane that "the
only way to advance the argument over the fruitfulness of
one way of looking at the field, compared to another, is to
come to grips with what others have said about it." And
second, Lane had "always thought that one of the virtues
of the behavioral approach is the intimate relation between

theory and data; each helps the other. This is a theoretical book, but there are no references to the studies which inform it, or which illuminate and illustrate the points made. Eulau has chosen to argue his case without showing what the behavioral approach can do."[2]

Lane was both right and wrong. He was wrong in that, as I still insist, a forced march through the labyrinth of scholarly research, overburdened with charts, tables, and statistics, is not conducive to communication with the student. He was right in that a book of empirical readings—which I had planned to prepare, and finally did bring out[3]—is useful; but, as I pointed out then, and would point out again here, it is best to leave it up to the instructor to choose from the relevant empirical material what he might consider conducive to learning.

Lane's review also raised a point that, in fact, informs the rationale behind this, the present volume. Feeling a simple explication would be more effective in my own communication with the student, I did not choose, in that first volume, to advance the argument for behavioralism in politics by "coming to grips with what others have said about it." But I have, however indirectly, done so here by inviting the student to make that confrontation.

Here the student will meet articulate exponents of several points of view, each a thoughtful, thought-provoking theorist responsible in some part for the way we now think of the political life. Professors Easton, Truman, Dahl, Strauss, Bay, and Merkl—all have my thanks for giving me permission to use their essays in this volume.

NOTES

1. *The Behavioral Persuasion in Politics* (New York: Random House, 1963).
2. *American Political Science Review,* 58 (March 1964), 105.
3. *Political Behavior in America: New Directions* (New York: Random House, 1966).

Contents

Preface   ix

Tradition and Innovation: On the Tension
between Ancient and Modern Ways in
the Study of Politics   1
HEINZ EULAU

1 : *The Condition of American Political Science*   22
DAVID EASTON

2 : *The Impact on Political Science of the Revolution*
in the Behavioral Sciences   38
DAVID B. TRUMAN

3 : *The Behavioral Approach in Political Science:*
Epitaph for a Monument to a Successful Protest   68
ROBERT A. DAHL

4 : *What Is Political Philosophy?*
The Problem of Political Philosophy   93
LEO STRAUSS

5 : *Politics and Pseudopolitics: A Critical Evaluation of Some Behavioral Literature*   109
CHRISTIAN BAY

6 : *"Behavioristic" Tendencies in American Political Science*   141
PETER H. MERKL

Index   153

BEHAVIORALISM IN POLITICAL SCIENCE

Tradition and Innovation: On the Tension between Ancient and Modern Ways in the Study of Politics

HEINZ EULAU

Changes in the thought-ways of science are usually accompanied by lively intellectual conflicts between opposing or divergent points of view. Indeed, the clash of ideas is probably a major ingredient of whatever it is that stimulates the life of the mind in whatever manifestation of human culture. Although for some self-appointed custodians of the Truth such conflicts are often a source of despair, it is in the crucible of arguments and counter-arguments, of proofs and disproofs, that changes in the arts and sciences take place.

In the last thirty years or so, but more intensively in the years since the Second World War, the study of politics has been rocked by disagreements over its scope, theories, and methods. Although these disagreements were no more and perhaps somewhat less frequent than in most sciences, natural or behavioral, they were at times conspicuously bitter and tendentious. It may be that the subject matter of political

1

science—politics and all that is involved in politics—has a kind of halo effect: because the stakes of politics make men fight and sometimes die for what they claim as their due, political scientists seem to confuse academic with political stakes, behaving as if the victories and defeats on the battleground of the intellect resemble those on the battleground of political life.

But we can also look at the controversies of the last few years in a different light. Perhaps they indicate that political scientists take their work seriously and expect it to have serious consequences for the course of events in the real world of politics. In this perspective, the debates suggest that political scientists have a profound sense of personal responsibility for the effects of their discoveries on the shape and quality of public affairs. It may be that this sense of responsibility is greater than the impact of political science on the real world of politics warrants. But it is there, and its being there might well be taken into account if one seeks to understand the dedication and commitment of the scholarly warriors.

On close inspection one would find that the controversies in political science cover a wide range of topics. But, for better or for worse, they have tended to be harnessed together under a single label—"behaviorism" or "behavioralism." As a result of this reduction of many controversies to the single issue, the identification of "sides" has not always been easy. And, in fact, no such identification has ever been successful. Nevertheless, by the late sixties, it has become reasonably clear that most of the controversies, whatever their immediate topics, have involved what one may call, as in so many other fields of cultural endeavor, "the battle of the ancients versus the moderns." The real issue, it turns out, is the issue of tradition and innovation in scientific development.

Again, this is not to say that the "traditionalists" have been united, opposing the new tendencies for the sake of tradition, or that the "innovators" have been united, promoting the new trends for the sake of innovation. In fact, as the controversies have unfolded and hitherto unspoken premises are clarified in the course of debate, it has not been uncommon to find common ground between some of the ancients and some of the moderns.

Intellectual battle lines, then, are not clear. Nevertheless, three issues seem critical: First, there has been disagreement over the nature of the knowledge of political things—is a science of politics possible, or is the study of politics a matter of philosophy? Second, and closely related to the first issue, there has been controversy over the place of values in the study of politics—a controversy that makes for a great deal of confusion. And third, there has been disagreement over the basic units of analysis in the study of politics—should the political scientist study individual and collective behavior, or should he limit himself to the study of institutions and large-scale processes? There are other controversies, and there are differing points of view and points of departure within the newer study of political behavior and political sociology. But, in general, the main issues have been the nature of political knowledge, the place of values, and the choice of units of analysis.

It is the purpose of this collection of essays to bring together at least some of the writings that, in the recent past, have sought to come to grips with these issues. Yet, strangely enough, in searching for relevant and worthwhile selections, I was astounded by the paucity of appropriate materials. There were some that might have been included but were not because they were expository of the behavioral persuasion rather than argumentative.[1] And there were others that might have been chosen but were not because they were, at the other extreme, so disengaged that the debaters, rather than talking to each other, only succeeded in talking past each other.[2]

But even if one takes these and other writings into account, it seems that many of the controversies over behavioralism in political science have been subterranean—fought out at professional conferences or within university departments rather than in the printed communication media. Just why this has been the case is difficult to say, and I can speak with reasonable confidence only about the attitude of those on the behavioral side. I remember a conversation with the late Morton Grodzins in the early fifties after a particularly frustrating round-table session at an annual meeting of the American Political Science Association. It was his position that we should minimize fruitless debates with our antagonists and, instead, get on with the empirical research—for much work was to be done—and not let ourselves be derailed by futile controversy. The burden of proof, he felt, was on us to produce the kind of work that, sooner or later, would find acceptance on its merits. Of course, complete disengagement was impossible, and from time to time it would be necessary to speak out. But the position that Grodzins took is of interest because it reveals why leading practitioners of the new political science sought to avoid being drawn into an endless *Methodenstreit*. Perhaps most suggestive in this respect was their reception of an ill-tempered attack on their work by a number of political philosophers of the school of Leo Strauss.[3] They remained silent while the counterattack was mounted by two political theorists who could hardly be suspected of being mouthpieces of the behavioral movement.[4] But Grodzins' position also bespoke the enormous optimism that he and others brought to the empirical research enterprise. The spirit of these years was to get on with the work, confident in the belief that the innovative tendencies would surely prevail.

In part, the silence of the behavior-oriented, empirical researchers was filled by David Easton in a book that after a lukewarm reception has come to have considerable impact on the direction of political science.[5] Easton thoroughly castigated the discipline for its theoretical antiquarianism, its methodological backwardness, its failure to march at the frontiers of inquiry alongside the behavioral sciences. Easton's view of the state of the discipline was widely shared by the generation for which he spoke. Not that all of us agreed with his pessimism, his tendency to reify concepts, his demand for autonomous theory, his quest for global rather than limited models, or his position on the relationship between political science and public policy. But his general critique of the discipline fell on willing ears, and once he had spoken there was little else to be said.

If Easton spoke for the theorists who found the established political science wanting, so David Truman spoke for those more empirically oriented researchers who had been so greatly influenced by Charles E. Merriam and his colleagues at the University of Chicago during the twenties and thirties. Unlike the disaffected theorists, this group was somewhat closer to the ongoing political process and had, perhaps, a somewhat firmer grasp of political reality. As Truman made clear in a widely appreciated essay on the changing focus of political science, to pose the issue of ancient and modern ways of doing things in terms of "institutional" versus "behavioral" analysis was neither necessary nor desirable.[6] And subsequent developments have confirmed Truman's diagnosis: The issue of behavioralism versus institutionalism has largely disappeared.

Both institutionalists and behavioralists have discovered their common commitment to the empirical investigation of political phenomena, and have discovered that just as an institution is not something independent of behavior, so behavior is not something independent of an institutional setting. Neglect of institutional or situational context, just as neglect of social behavior, was likely to distort the scientific perception of political reality. Political behaviorists have come to realize that in attempting to explain the varieties of political behavior, institutions provide their own methodological advantages.

It may be useful to illustrate the convergence of institu-

tional and behavioral analysis by referring to two pieces of
research published, within the short span of two years, in
1960 and 1962. In their remarkable *The American Voter*
(1960) the individual voter was the unit of analysis for Angus
Campbell and his associates, but they utilized the data gathered at the level of the individual to develop a suggestive
theory of elections as institutionalized events at the system
level of analysis.[7] On the other hand, in *The Legislative System* (1962), John C. Wahlke and his colleagues began with
the institutional setting of the legislature as the given, explored the variety of attitudes and roles, norms and relationships of individual legislators, and concluded with a
description of the institution as a system of highly patterned
behavior.[8] If one contrasts either work with earlier studies,
behavioralist or "traditional," of voting behavior or of legislative bodies, the convergence in scientific outlook is marked
indeed.

A similar convergence of what were at one time considered
ancient and modern ways of political inquiry occurred in
the controversy over synchronic versus diachronic analysis.
On the one hand, charges were not uncommon that historical
studies of political events or of institutional or policy developments were of purely antiquarian interest and failed to
take account of contemporary theoretical and methodological
advances—in short, that they failed to contribute to the
growth of a science of politics. On the other hand, studies
of political behavior, and especially those dependent on the
survey as the instrument of data collection, were criticized
for lack of historical depth and long-range significance.
Once more two works of the sixties may serve to illustrate
how this particular controversy has been buried. In his *Who
Governs?* (1962), Robert A. Dahl was primarily interested
in discovering the distribution of influence in an American
city at the time of inquiry.[9] But he provided a rich historical
background by tracing the circulation of the city's elite
through time and combining it with case analyses of several

policy-making arenas and a cross-sectional study of resource distribution among the population. And in *The Rulers and the Ruled* (1964), Robert E. Agger and his associates combined a comparative, cross-sectional analysis of power relationships in four communities with an ingenious technique for coping with the problem of comparing the developmental stages of political change.[10] By providing a high degree of historical depth to their analysis without being "historical," these authors demonstrated that there is no necessary conflict between behavioral and historical methods.

Only eight years had passed after Easton's 1953 complaint about the "malaise" of political science when Robert Dahl could write an "epitaph for a monument to a successful protest."[11] Taking a long look at what had happened in political science and how it had happened, Dahl was pleased. What he said, in effect, was that the old political science was dead. It would be idle to speculate whether the behavioral mood, as Dahl called it, had conquered political science, or whether it had been coopted by political science. The consequence, as Dahl saw it, was the same. But perhaps more symbolic of the changed state of affairs was the fact that Dahl's epitaph was not disputed. It seems to me that it should have been, for even today it strikes me as unduly optimistic. If scientific development in the social sciences were as linear and cumulative as it is in the natural and physical sciences, Dahl's optimism would be appropriate. But, I fear, though cumulation is certainly a desirable goal of a science of politics, it is not in fact characteristic of the social sciences. As I said on another occasion:

> The history of political science as an independent field of inquiry can be written as a history of successive emancipations from earlier limitations and false starts. Yet, these successive emancipations have been additive rather than cumulative: the old survives with the new, and the old acquires new defenders as the new relies on old apostles. It is impossible to say, therefore, that anything has been disproven as long as conventional

tests of proof—the requisites of scientific status in any field of knowledge—are not commonly accepted by political scientists, or, in fact, are rejected by some as altogether irrelevant in political inquiry.[12]

To put this somewhat differently, it seems to me that the social sciences are characterized by an immanent tension between tradition and innovation, between the ancient and the modern. In the social sciences traditional ways of doing things have a power to survive that is quite unlike the situation in the natural sciences. This is not to say that this need be the case. I am saying that it is the case, whether we like it or not. I expect, therefore, that the traditional ways of legal-institutional, historical, rational-speculative analysis that have come down to us from the Greeks and Romans will continue to be practiced by scholarly students of politics. To argue that the work of those who cherish these approaches is inferior strikes me as inappropriate. Because what they are doing is different from what the behavioral scientists are doing does not mean that one or the other approach is superior. But it does mean, I think, that there will be continued tension in the academic study of politics between ancient and modern ways of thought.

My own interpretation of what has happened in political science differs from Dahl's, then, in that I see the behavioral movement more as a successful renaissance than as a successful revolution. It is in the nature of a renaissance to look both forward and backward, to seek out what seems worthwhile in the past in order to shape a more viable future. The behavioral persuasion has come to be recognized as an integral part of the established political science rather than as a new establishment. It has come to be recognized not because its models and methods are somehow "right" and other approaches "wrong" but because it has produced excellent work at the frontiers of the study of politics. It would be folly to claim that only behavioral scientists can do good work on politics. There are behavioral studies of politics, perhaps more than one might wish for, that are bad, just as there are traditional or conventional studies that are good by their own standards of excellence. It would be hybris to believe that the behavioral-scientific movement will drive the more traditional ways of studying politics out of the temple of political science. Intellectual obsolescence is always around the corner, and the behavioral persuasion in the study of politics is not immune.

Lest I be accused of a sweet reasonableness that is neither my temperament nor my goal, let me turn to Leo Strauss' critique of the new political science. For this critique represents, better than any other, the "ancient" ways of seeing political phenomena. His essay on "What Is Political Philosophy?" is remarkable because it joins clearly the issues of knowledge and values in the study of politics.[13] Strauss attacked behavioralism—as he interpreted it—as a form of positivism that seeks a "value-free" political science. There is no need for me to summarize Strauss' arguments, for no one speaks as well for his point of view as Strauss himself. But because behavioralists have all too often given short shrift to the Straussian argument, let me say that his point of view should be given more attention; for precisely because he is partially correct in his diagnosis of the issues, what is objectionable in his argument deserves scrutiny.

That opinion should be replaced by knowledge, that philosophy is not in possession but in quest of truth, that political philosophy "is the attempt truly to know both the nature of political things and the right, or the good, political order," that political philosophy ought to be distinguished from political thought, theory, and theology as well as from political science—all of these propositions make sense. And no one has, I think, more discerningly articulated the difference between the general conception of political science and his own view of what political philosophy is all about. "To understand the meaning" of what "useful work" is done by political scientists, Strauss asks us to remember that "political philosophy is the attempt to understand the nature of political things." In a paragraph that appears in the book version of his essay but was not included in the earlier journal version, he writes:

> Before one can even think of attempting to understand the nature of political things, one must know political things: one must possess political knowledge. At least every sane adult possesses political knowledge to some degree. Everyone knows something about taxes, police, law, jails, war, peace, armistice. Everyone knows that the aim of war is victory, that war demands the supreme sacrifice and many other deprivations, that bravery deserves praise and cowardice deserves blame.[14]

Now, if I understand Strauss correctly, and I have honestly tried to do so, the method of political philosophy that he advocates is this: first, to assume the truth of common-sense knowledge as set forth in the paragraph just quoted; second, to lay bare through intuitive thought processes the "assumptions which concern not merely the given political situation, but political life or human life as such"; and third, to subject these assumptions to "critical and coherent analysis."

But, Strauss argues, political philosophy is in a state of decay. The culprit is a perverted kind of positivism which, toward the end of the last century,

> reached its final form by realizing or decreeing that there is a fundamental difference between facts and values, and that only factual statements are within the competence of science: scientific social science is incompetent to pronounce value judgments, and must avoid value judgments altogether.[15]

From this point onward Strauss' argument becomes a series of *non sequiturs:* first, "moral obtuseness is the necessary condition for scientific analysis"; second, "the more serious we are as social scientists, the more completely we develop within ourselves a state of indifference to any goal, or of aimlessness and drifting, a state which may be called nihilism"; and third, according to the social scientist's principles, "truth is not a value which it is necessary to choose: one may reject it as well as choose it."

I find these statements interesting because they seem to reveal a very low level of tolerance for ambiguity. "Ethical neutrality" is, for some social scientists, a desirable intellectual stance precisely because of the impossibility of *logically* deriving values from facts, and not because social scientists are insensitive to values and goals. Strauss, insensitive to facts, does not see it that way. "Ethical neutrality," he argues, is "an alibi for thoughtlessness and vulgarity." And, therefore, "social science positivism fosters not so much nihilism as conformism and philistinism."[16]

Most reasonable men would agree, I think, that a line of argument that alternately accuses the social scientist of nihilism as well as of conformism and philistinism does not sound very convincing; Strauss has, in fact, failed to convince many outside his personal circle of disciples, and he has certainly failed to stem the tide of behavioralism in political science. He has failed because his method of arriving at the truth does not recognize empirical reality and does not permit intersubjective validation of that reality. Part of this reality is the fact that social scientists as they live and work are neither contemptuous of values nor disinterested in public policies. Gabriel A. Almond once put it succinctly in an earlier debate when he stated that because "science cannot create values," it does not follow that scientists cannot investigate values if they wish to do so, that they cannot concern themselves with the consequences of alternate policy choices, or that they cannot become active participants in the game (or struggle, as some prefer to call it) of politics.[17]

Unlike Strauss, most social scientists are sensitive to the possibility that commitment to a value position may create moral problems that cannot easily be solved. If I understand the position of most contemporary behavioral scientists correctly, there is general agreement on the following three aspects of the value problem. First, on the question of whether values can and should be studied by the methods of science, the answer is an unequivocal "yes," just as the answer is "yes" to the question of whether behavioral science can assess the consequences of alternate policy choices. Second, on the question of whether a "value-free" social science is possible, the answer is "no," though the exclusion of value considerations in the form of biases that distort scientific inquiry is desirable. And third, on the question of whether behavioral science can arrive at judgments of what is "good" and what is "bad," the answer is that it cannot—that such judgments are, indeed, the task of ethics as a separate enterprise.

This leaves a fourth question—the question of the behavioral scientist's own involvement in the issues of the day. Here behavioral scientists disagree, and their disagreement, stemming from the nature of science itself, is profound. For there is nothing in the *logic* of science that compels the scientist to commit himself to one of several conflicting public purposes—or to withhold his commitment. Commitment is as defensible as its opposite. Of course, noncommitment as well as commitment is a moral position, and the scientist who fails to commit himself on public issues is, in the end, as responsible for his noncommitment as the involved scientist is for his involvement. In this respect, then, the scientist must come to terms with his own moral conscience. Neither science nor philosophy can legislate his course of action.

But all of what I have said about the place of values in behavioral science and the role of the behavioral scientist is predicated on one fundamental assumption which all scientists who are true to science must make. The assumption is that science can function only in an environment that permits freedom of inquiry and freedom of speech. For where the condition of freedom does not exist, scientific investigation, as we commonly think of it, cannot function according to its own canons of method and procedure. Only if the scientist is a free man can he perform his work, and only if he is a free man can he make the moral choice of participating in or abstaining from political life. I would argue, therefore, that in this respect, at least, science itself dictates a moral choice. Hence the scientist must be forever vigilant lest the freedoms necessary for his scientific work be infringed upon. In this connection, then, the modern scientist, whether natural or behavioral, carries on his shoulders the burden of an ancient problem.

There is no better example of the tension between ancient aspirations and modern limitations than Christian Bay's essay on "Politics and Pseudopolitics."[18] If the Straussians discover in Plato and Aristotle the right *answers,* which need only be applied to contemporary issues, Bay discovers in Plato and Aristotle the right *question*—"above all, what is politics *for?*" A political science that does not ask this question is what Bay calls "pseudopolitics." So far, so good. But Bay also rejects as pseudopolitics the answer that politics is concerned "with promoting private or private interest-group advantage." Politics, once more, becomes a definitional game, an approach that does not really solve anything. His attack on pseudopolitics simply implies Bay's own preference for a definition of the political as "all activity aimed at improving or protecting conditions for the satisfaction of human needs and demands in a given society or community, according to some universalistic scheme of priorities, implicit or explicit."

There are two things to be said about this definition of politics by arbitrary restriction. In the first place, much political activity throughout history has been directed toward the achievements of goals that were eminently evil. To neglect this kind of politics would deprive the study of politics of some of its most perplexing problems.

But second, Bay's quest for some "universalistic scheme" for ordering choices among conflicting needs and demands is truly ancient. The task of behavioral science presumably is to discover these needs and translate them into an actionable agenda for the improvement of social conditions. I have no objection to anyone's pursuing such a program of research and reform. But the implicit notion that "right" courses of action can be derived from behavioral inquiry into human needs and then be employed to determine worthwhile topics for behavioral research is circular. I suspect that any proposed "universalistic scheme" for ordering needs and values would be nothing less than a modern version of the "closed society." The spell of Plato seems to be pervasive indeed. Bay's conception of politics illustrates well the tension between tradition and innovation in political science, even if, as is here the case, or perhaps because it is the case, the research program that is advocated would lie at the frontiers of behavioral inquiry.

It would be aesthetically satisfying if one could point to some over-all convergence in the conceptions of a behavioral science of politics that would transcend the variety of different points of view. Yet, this seems to be a hopeless task. Indeed, I believe that to search for a comprehensive schema is to chase a phantom. I doubt that a science of politics will be advanced by arguing, on purely theoretical grounds, for "central organizing concepts" such as system, power, communication, or decision making. And I doubt that it is possible to combine these partial approaches in some grand synthesis. A science is advanced by its tangible research discoveries and not by conceptual frameworks, models, or theories alone. These things, along with methods and techniques, are the tools of scientific inquiry. Whether they are scientifically viable can be determined only in the crucible of empirical research.

This is not to say that empirical research at the level of individual behavior should proceed without theoretical directions that are relevant to the macro concerns of political science. On the contrary, only if behavioral research at the micro level is cast in some theoretical frame of reference that relates it to large-scale processes or situations can it claim to be contributing to the solution of politically significant problems. There have been works of this order,* yet, despite the renaissance in the study of politics in the last decade or so, the output of creative empirical work remains disappointing, and this is particularly true of those subfields of the discipline that deal with comparative or international politics. It is all the more important to realize, therefore, that what will make the study of politics "scientific" is not theory but adherence to the canons of scientific method in collecting evidence and moving from there to inference. Not the theory as such, but the theory's derivative and empirically tested hypotheses explain those uniformities, regularities, and relationships that a science of politics assumes to exist.

Although the goal of scientific work is nothing less than the achievement of universal validity for its propositions, I doubt that a theory of "politics as such" is, at least for the present and immediate future, a feasible research strategy. Put differently, I believe that theorizing carried out in the context of empirical research is more useful in the current state of the social sciences. The difference in style of theorizing between "pure" theorists in search of universal propositions and "contextual" theorists ready to settle for partial explanations is, I think, once more symptomatic of the tension between the ancient and the modern modes of thought. My point is not that one group follows ancient and the other modern ways; but rather that the ancient quest for

---

* One might cite *The Civic Culture* by Gabriel A. Almond and Sidney Verba; *The Rulers and the Ruled* by Robert E. Agger and his associates; *Public Opinion and American Democracy* by V. O. Key; *Who Governs?* by Robert A. Dahl; *Political Ideology* by Robert E. Lane; *The American Voter* by Angus Campbell and his team; *The Legislative System* by John C. Wahlke and colleagues; *American Business and Public Policy* by Raymond A. Bauer and collaborators; *Political Parties: A Behavioral Analysis* by Samuel J. Eldersveld; *The Power of the Purse* by Richard F. Fenno, Jr.; *The American System* by the late Morton Grodzins; or *Negroes and the New Southern Politics* by Donald R. Matthews and James W. Prothro.

universal truth still permeates modern approaches and makes for the tension that is probably immanent in the study of man and his works.

In particular, I see a manifestation of the tension between tradition and innovation in the current popularity of systemic and functional analysis, of one kind or another, at the level of macro phenomena. Involved here is the ancient commitment to explaining, on the one hand, "wholes," and, on the other hand, a discomfort with positivism in science. Because human action is purposive and goal oriented, the possibility of an altogether positive behavioral political science is indeed questionable. But because human action is purposive, does it follow that "systems as wholes" are also purposive? To attribute goals and purposes to "systems or wholes" is, from the behavioral perspective, to ignore the purely analytic quality of such concepts. The attribution is, therefore, untenable, but because invariably the system or whole turns out to be the "state" of old—the concrete, empirical collectivity that is, in fact, a very real actor in the arena of politics. No wonder, then, that a concern with "system as whole" continues to fascinate the imagination of students of comparative or international politics for whom the nation-state remains an important unit of analysis. Since the human collectivity is an actor with actionable ends-in-view, the analytic system that presumably explains the behavior of the collectivity—be it primitive tribe or supranational organization —is endowed with goal-oriented functions which, it is said, "must" be performed if the system is to maintain itself and achieve its objectives. Yet, these functions—say the socialization of the membership or the aggregation of demands— cannot be disconfirmed. There is, then, in the functional formulations of systems, a teleological element that is prescientific or meta-theoretical in the ways of the ancients rather than scientific and empirical-theoretical in the ways of the moderns.

Admittedly, it is difficult not to think in functional terms, and the issue is certainly not the truth or falsity of functional formulations but their utility. However, to demonstrate the utility of functional formulations, they must be translated into causal propositions of the conditions under which uniformities, regularities, or relationships can be expected to occur. For scientific research can test only causal, not teleological, hypotheses. A proposition such as "the more successful a group is in inducing new members, the more loyal will its members be in time of stress" can be empirically tested. A proposition such as "every political system must socialize its members in order to survive in time of stress" is not testable because it cannot be falsified. The proposition is a meta-theoretical statement that is true by definition, for if applied to a concrete group, a group is by definition a set of persons who have been socialized into the group.

Behavioralism may be unequivocal in its choice of the individual as the empirical unit of analysis, but there is no agreement on the basic theoretical unit. At least two major approaches have crystallized in the last few years. On the one hand, there are those who, pointing to the basic *social* nature of man, see interindividual relationships and inter-actions—summarized in the concept of role—as the relevant theoretical point of departure. On the other hand, there are those who, influenced by classical economics, treat the individual not only as the empirical but also—in the model of the rational, self-interested, calculating, and utility-maximizing man—as the theoretical unit of analysis.[19] Implicit in these differing approaches are fundamentally different views of reality. The "sociological" approach, if it is proper to name it so, sees politics as a set of ordered relations among people, whereas the so-called "economic" approach sees politics as a set of rules or strategies by which individuals order their relationships.

The two approaches, however, are by no means mutually exclusive. The individualism of the "economists" is methodological and not substantive. True, some "economists" come at times dangerously close to mistaking the self-seeking, utility-maximizing motivations of the individuals of their theory for "real" motivations. But no such imputation is necessary. The assumption of the rational actor may be empirically false, but it can have great predictive power and generate hypotheses that can be empirically tested; true, also, that the approach of the "economists" is frankly normative and activist, yet dependent on rigorous and precise methods of deduction. It is very persuasive because it permits prediction and, therefore, orients behavior to action.

On the other hand, the "sociologists" prefer to proceed from behavioral assumptions more in line with empirical reality, and they are more inclined to employ methods of induction for the purpose of explanation rather than prediction. Not surprisingly, the "sociologists" are more interested in discovering the causes and consequences of behavior than in charting new avenues of political action.

There is built into the dialogue of these two approaches of behavioral political science the tension between ancient and modern ways of thought, but it is not likely to be conflictual. Surely, explanation—the goal of the ancients—is not an alternative to prediction—the hope of the moderns. Sooner or later, as in Herbert Simon's model of "satisficing man," a more realistic assumption about human behavior comes to find a place in a rational theory of action. On the other hand, as in some recent works by Peter Blau or Gerhard Lenski, deductive, if cautious, theorizing is used in seeking to explain complex, multi-causal empirical phenomena.[20]

Perhaps it is best to think of the study of politics as an ever expanding set of concentric circles, with a core that undergoes change very slowly, if at all, and with a periphery that is ill-defined and forever changing. At the core we find the most traditional of approaches—the speculative, philosophical stance invented by Socrates and Plato, which still has such a strong hold on scholars of the school of Leo

Strauss. Here the search is for Truth, with a capital "T," and for eternal knowledge. At the periphery we encounter the agenda of behavioral science which, unlike any other agenda, knows no limits. It knows no limits because the method of science does not know final knowledge. Here inquiry is undertaken as much to reduce ignorance as to discover truth. What knowledge emerges is assumed to be partial, possibly temporary, contingent on the state of science, and always probabilistic. As science reduces ignorance, it may know what is not the case; it does not arrogate to itself knowledge of the truth. In this sense, behavioral science is without firm boundaries and its agenda is never exhausted.

If this image of political science is at all viable, it gives us a clue to understanding the tension between tradition and innovation that I feel characterizes the discipline. On the one hand, there remains at the core of political inquiry that quest for certainty that made the wisdom of Socrates so influential an ingredient of the Western tradition. On the other hand, there is the revolutionary potential that is inherent in the methods of modern behavioral science, but that is prepared to settle for probability. I do not believe that by some magic dialectic thesis and antithesis will merge into a future synthesis. On the contrary, I see the goings-on at the core and at the periphery as unalterably opposed to each other, yet bound to each other by virtue of their common concern with the commonwealth. Peter Merkl's measured appraisal of the behavioral movement[21] confirms my suspicion that not all of political science is ready to surrender to the behavioral approaches. But if my model of political science as a set of concentric circles bound to each other in a tension that arises out of the dialectic between core and periphery has any merit at all, Merkl's standpoint, much as one might dissent from it in particulars, is likely to be conducive to re-establishing the dialogue between the hinterland of tradition and the frontiers of innovation in the study of politics.

REFERENCES

1. See, for instance, Austin Ranney, ed., *Essays on the Behavioral Study of Politics* (Urbana: University of Illinois Press, 1962).
2. See, for instance, James C. Charlesworth, ed., *The Limits of Behavioralism in Political Science* (Philadelphia: American Academy of Political and Social Science, 1962); and James C. Charlesworth, ed., *A Design for Political Science: Scope, Objectives, and Methods* (Philadelphia: American Academy of Political and Social Science, 1966).
3. Herbert J. Storing, ed., *Essays on the Scientific Study of Politics* (New York: Holt, Rinehart & Winston, 1962).
4. John H. Schaar and Sheldon S. Wolin, "Essays on the Scientific Study of Politics: A Critique," *American Political Science Review,* 57 (March 1963), 125–50.
5. David Easton, *The Political System: An Inquiry into the State of Political Science* (New York: Alfred A. Knopf, 1953). A selection from this book is reprinted below, chapter 1.
6. David B. Truman, "The Impact on Political Science of the Revolution in the Behavioral Sciences," in *Research Frontiers in Politics and Government* (Washington, D.C.: Brookings Institution, 1955), pp. 202–31. Reprinted below, chapter 2.
7. Angus Campbell, Philip E. Converse, Warren E. Miller, and Donald E. Stokes, *The American Voter* (New York: John Wiley, 1960).
8. John C. Wahlke, Heinz Eulau, William Buchanan, and LeRoy C. Ferguson, *The Legislative System: Explorations in Legislative Behavior* (New York: John Wiley, 1962).
9. Robert A. Dahl, *Who Governs? Democracy and Power in an American City* (New Haven: Yale University Press, 1961).
10. Robert E. Agger, Daniel Goldrich, and Bert E. Swanson, *The Rulers and the Ruled: Political Power and Impotence in American Communities* (New York: John Wiley, 1964).
11. Robert A. Dahl, "The Behavioral Approach in Political Science: Epitaph for a Monument to a Successful Protest," *American Political Science Review,* 55 (December 1961), 763–72. Reprinted below, chapter 3.
12. Heinz Eulau, "Political Science," in Bert F. Hoselitz, ed., *A Reader's Guide to the Social Sciences* (New York: The Free Press, 1959), p. 94.
13. Leo Strauss, "What Is Political Philosophy?", *Journal of Politics,* 19 (August 1957), 343–68. Part I of this essay, "The Problem of Political Philosophy," is reprinted below, chapter 4.
14. Leo Strauss, *What Is Political Philosophy?* (New York: The Free Press, 1959), p. 14.
15. *Ibid.,* p. 18.
16. *Ibid.,* p. 20.

17. Gabriel A. Almond, "Politics, Science, and Ethics," *American Political Science Review,* 40 (1946), 283–93.
18. Christian Bay, "Politics and Pseudopolitics: A Critical Evaluation of Some Behavioral Literature," *American Political Science Review,* 59 (March 1965), 39–51. Reprinted below, chapter 5.
19. See, for instance, James M. Buchanan and Gordon Tullock, *The Calculus of Consent* (Ann Arbor: University of Michigan Press, 1962).
20. Peter M. Blau, *Exchange and Power in Social Life* (New York: John Wiley and Sons, 1964); Gerhard Lenski, *Power and Privilege: A Theory of Social Stratification* (New York: McGraw-Hill, 1965).
21. Peter Merkl, "Behavioristische Tendenzen in der amerikanischen Politischen Wissenschaft, *Politische Vierteljahresschrift,* 6 (March 1965), 58–86. Chapter 6 is a translated adaption of this article.

1 ⠿ The Condition of American Political Science

DAVID EASTON

Since the Civil War, American political science has come a long way in company with other social sciences. In the last quarter of the nineteenth century it was scarcely discernible as a separate teaching or research discipline.[1] While there are no exact data on the number of college and university instructors devoting most of their time to the study and teaching of politics, one author suggests that in 1900 they did not exceed a hundred.[2] As late as 1914 a typical large university offered at most twenty courses devoted to political science; and in a sample of three hundred universities and colleges, only thirty-eight maintained separate departments for the study of politics.[3]

Today the figures alone testify to the tremendous strides taken in political research. Full-time teachers of the subject exceed a thousand and the number of teachers engaged in

Reprinted from *The Political System* (New York: Alfred A. Knopf, 1953), pp. 38–52, by permission of the author and the publisher.

one way or another in teaching it reaches almost five thousand.[4] It is not unusual to find the larger universities each offering thirty to forty courses in the subject. Certainly no university or college of repute could afford to be without an administratively independent department of political science. This numerical strength of political science and its crystallization as a discipline are simply an index of the vast corps of workers now available for inquiry into the various aspects of domestic and international relations. Research has in fact ranged from the minute problems of personnel selection for municipal government to the unbounded horizons of international conflict, and from the activity of the individual in local politics to the interaction of national collectivities in a world society.

This wealth of accessible knowledge has helped to carry the political scientist into the turbulent stream of policy formation. At the turn of the century, training in political science alone was seldom sufficient to bring an invitation from official public agencies for consultation. Statesmen, complained Lowell early in the century, do not turn to professors of political science for advice.[5] Today the ties between national or state capitols and university circles are strong and numerous. The historic report of the President's Committee on Administrative Management was almost exclusively the work of specialists with formal training in political science; and the recent Hoover Commission on the Organization of the Executive Branch of Government drew heavily upon their knowledge. The frustrating fact, for many political scientists, that their advice about means has often fallen on deaf ears is as much a commentary on the vagaries of policy conflicts within the political process as on the validity of the suggestions. It is true that with the exception of public administration, formal education in political science has not achieved the recognition in government circles accorded, say, economics or psychology.[6] Nevertheless, the demands made on political scientists during the recent war were heavy enough to raise the question in not a few universities as to where the immediate obligation of the teacher in political science lay, to his students or to his government.

Yet, in spite of undeniable accomplishments, and in spite of the fact that every year there are millions of valuable and talented man-hours devoted to political research and its communication to others, the condition of American political science is disturbing and disappointing, if not in absolute results at least in terms of what is possible. That it falls short of what is needed is not subject to dispute; that it has failed to maximize its inherent and available potentialities is a more controversial matter.

To each generation its crucial political problems seem never to have been matched before; nevertheless, by any measure, a civilization has seldom been faced with a crisis weighted with graver consequences than that confronting us today. In the face of an urgent need for some reliable knowledge as an aid in solving our perplexities, whatever the enthusiasm and admiration for the present accomplishments of political research, honesty would compel an unimpassioned observer to confess that the fund of political knowledge falls far short of what is required. Other social sciences can still offer little enough; the whole corpus of social research is at so early a stage in its growth. Over twenty years ago Frederic Ogg complained in a biting evaluation of the trends in social research that "the meagerness of first-rate American contributions to philosophy, philology, political science . . . reveals the immaturity of our culture. Plenty of research work, of a kind, is all the time in progress. Quantitatively, there is little ground for complaint. But a considerable proportion of the studies undertaken are ill-planned, crudely executed, and barren of significant result."[7] Since that date great strides have been taken in the study of politics, but it lags far behind the other social sciences.

If the condition of political science represented the exhaustion of its present potentialities, then there would be little justification in voicing any concern about it. But comparison with the level of achievement of other social sciences demonstrates what political science could be doing. However much students of political life may seek to escape the taint, if they were to eavesdrop on the whisperings of their fellow social scientists, they would find that they are almost generally stigmatized as the least advanced. They could present society, they would hear, with at least a slice of bread but they offer it only a crumb. However hard this may fall on their ears, and however incendiary it may be to their professional pride, it must be the starting point for a forthright, even though at times distressing, discussion of the present condition of political science.

Political research has still to penetrate to the hard core of political power in society. Each revision or reaffirmation of social policy, if it is to be effective, must depend on reliable knowledge about the distribution of social power. Without this knowledge, there can be little assurance about the way in which political decisions will be formulated and about the degree to which, once adopted, they will be realized in practice. In spite of the intensive research activity of the last seventy-five years only limited knowledge can as yet be offered on the fundamental distribution of power among the basic social aggregates. Instead, in examining the way in which social groups interact in the creation and execution of policy, there has been a pronounced inclination in political research to assume the stability of the basic power pattern within which this interaction takes place. As a whole, political science has viewed the fundamental patterns of influence as given and has sought largely to trace the way in which the political process functions within this pattern. Not that it has disregarded the broader problem entirely, for there are numerous insights, supported with evidence in varying degrees, to suggest that the bulk of power lies with a political class, with the bureaucracy, or in some vague way with the people. But the energies of the discipline as a whole have not been given to developing consistent and integrated research in order that it might identify the major variables affecting power relations and the significant kinds of data to be observed. Solutions to these problems are inescapable prerequisites for the description of the basic power distribution in society.

However fashionable it may be today to talk about power and the power struggle, only occasionally have these lacunae in political research been observed. V. O. Key has complained that "the pattern of the allocation of values through politics has not been explored enough to permit ready collation" for a "study of politics as status [that] would furnish for a given moment a picture of the pattern of power and of the distribution of those ends or objectives that are gained through political power."[8] But research still concentrates on the trees.

Without reliable knowlege about the configurations of power, the determinants and knowable consequences of policy will continue to be vague and scientifically unforeseeable. Indeed, such is the state of political research that it is not uncommon to hear that many a Washington columnist has an intimate insight into and reliable knowledge of political life envied by most political scientists. The same cannot be said about the businessman's knowledge of economics or the visitor's insights into a foreign culture as compared with the respective generalizations of the economist or the cultural anthropologist. Unless political research is able to throw some light on the sources and knowable consequences of policy to give a more reliable picture than the insight of the well-informed layman—in this case the politician, the administrator, and those, like top-level columnists or lobbyists, whose job it is to know—the existence of a special political discipline will indeed take a good deal of explaining.

Not only is there a lack of knowledge about the locus of political power, but students of political life have also been prone to forget that the really crucial problems of social research are concerned with the patterns of change. No social institution is stationary; it is in continuous, if at times imperceptible, change. The idea of stationary conditions is an artificial abstraction necessary only as a means for simplifying changing reality. Its value lies in the fact that ultimately we shall be able to explain how we get from one moment to another in history. Yet, in spite of the acceptance as axiomatic, of Heraclitus's well-known propositions about change, over the last seventy-five years political research has confined itself largely to the study of given conditions to the neglect of political change.

Aside from a brief period in the twenties and thirties, when it was fashionable to study revolutions as climactic moments in a process of change, and with the further exception of a sporadic and minor interest in the genesis and course of political movements, political science has viewed its task as one of discovering how political institutions function today and what may happen in the immediate tomorrow. Although political scientists are taught to criticize fifth-century Greek thought for its dangerous and indeed fatal search for the conditions of stability, it is a tragedy of contemporary research that it too stands committed to the investigation of similar conditions. In fact, the preoccupation of contemporary political research with stationary conditions has even graver consequences than the similar preoccupation of the Greeks. The critical inclinations of the latter stand in marked contrast to the strong predisposition in American political research to view the going political system as though, with all its avowed imperfections, it were the best of all possible practical worlds. For this reason it is in Candide's tutor, Pangloss, not in the hypercritical Greeks, that we see the image in caricature of the modern political scientist.

Political research was not always thus chained to the present. In the great age of liberal speculation and inquiry, especially in the early nineteenth century, the going political

systems were always under the questioning scrutiny of skep-
tical social philosophers. As the work of any of the prominent nineteenth-century social philosophers, such as Comte
or Marx, illustrates, they were interested in projecting present trends into the future. They stood on top of their world
to see what a new world might be like; this was the occasion
for an abortive attempt to define the laws of social change.
Today political research seldom transcends the frame of reference of its own age. However painful it may be to admit,
political research leaves the impression that the study of the
sources and the direction of basic change is not of great
consequence or urgency.

Furthermore, if we look at this research for its exactness
of meaning and concreteness of reference, we find that here
too it is wanting. At the earliest stage in the growth of social
science, the stage out of which we may hope it is now passing, propositions are inevitably formulated as insights rather
than as research statements. The initial identification of relevant variables and their relationships is always the work of
a talented, uncurbed imagination.[9] At this exploratory stage
the important thing is to grope one's way to a vague and not
necessarily precise discovery of the vital elements and their
connections, to obtain the insights. The activity of the imagination here is largely a matter of art about which we know
little[10] and it is of course the difference between keen
imagination and pedestrian perception that separates the
great from the mediocre political scientist. But whatever tal-
ent the insights may mirror, the first stage in any social
science is clearly that of discovery, without too much concern for the rigor of the formulation of the propositions or
the precision of meaning of the concepts.

When we look at the greater part of political research
over the past several decades we cannot help but conclude
that it shows evidence of still being in this earliest stage and,
what is disturbing, it seems to be perpetuating this condition
today. It exerts little effort to raise itself to the next stage.

The major concepts, for example, are still frustratingly unclear. A science, it is often said, is as strong as its concepts;
and if this is true, the vague, ill-defined concepts unfortunately so typical of research in political science reduce the
discipline to a low position on a scale of maturity in the
social sciences.[11] It is the rule rather than the exception to
find difficulty in referring political concepts back to the things
to which presumably they refer.

Part of this difficulty results from the very scope of the
terms. Concepts such as "dictatorship," "class," "sover-
eignty," "responsibility,"[12] and the like convey such broad
meanings that it is possible for a number of students to use
them apparently with reference to the same social phenomena but in fact with reference to considerably different
things. In other cases the concepts such as "freedom," "liberty," "equality," "rights," "democracy," and so forth provide the additional difficulty of conveying both factual and
distinctly evaluative meanings in research which presumably
seeks to be primarily empirical. If, for empirical research,
we define a good concept as one that refers to an identifiable
set of facts and that can be explained in terms of the operations needed to discover these facts, then a good part of the
terminology used in political science falls far short of this
standard.

The imprecision of the concepts explains in large part the
reasons why there are such differences about political generalizations. With ambiguous terms the generalizations themselves
become very broad and vaguely worded; the consequence is
that definitive confirmation or invalidation for any given time
is impossible. One set of political scientists can argue that
planning and dictatorship are unalterably associated; another
can demonstrate the contrary. One can maintain that the separation of powers acts as a restraint on political power; another can prove that it really makes possible the capricious
and irresponsible exercise of power. It is possible to do for
the whole of political science what one student has done for

public administration; namely, to show that, like folk proverbs, for each principle supported by considerable evidence there is a contradictory one supportable by evidence of equal weight.[13] The result is that all too often we have propositions, the subjects and predicates of which are so poorly defined that the meticulous student of politics finds it impossible to judge between conflicting statements.

I do not intend these remarks to depreciate the value of existing political knowledge. On the contrary, traditional political science has attracted and continues to attract to its approach some of the brilliant minds of each generation. In consequence it could not help but offer penetrating insights into the nature of the political process and the operation of political institutions; nor could it fail to identify crucial variables that must be examined more systematically. Twenty-five years ago such knowledge was at the forefront of the social sciences. Today it is still vital. But political research has now reached a point where it is possible to take what are essentially insights, to refine them, and to begin to examine them more rigorously. It is not a matter of discarding or spurning the results of what has come to be called traditional political research. It is a matter, wherever possible, of using the available knowledge as the point of departure for the next stage of development, namely, to increase its reliability. Knowledge of method for the study of human activity has now made it mandatory and feasible, in preparation for this next period, to attack the problem of reformulating political knowledge with all the resources that can be spared or commanded, so that it becomes more easily verifiable. In this way it will become possible to determine which insights to reject or to accept as valid.

The value of social science ultimately rests in its attempt to transcend ordinary insight by testing it, and where it proves erroneous, by correcting it; and where, even when correct, it does not explain fully the phenomenon under scrutiny, by penetrating to deeper levels of understanding. If the experience of some of the social sciences, such as economics or psychology, or of the natural sciences is a guide, research such as this ultimately demands the gradual creation of a new meaningful vocabulary, to be distinguished from artificial and unnecessary jargon, the refinement of current concepts, and the development of special techniques for observing and reporting data, collating and testing them.

The search for these indicia of scientific sophistication in the study of political life is in vain. Most works on politics do not pass beyond the comprehension of the ordinary well-educated person, untutored in political science. This has a merit, of course, in that communication between the political scientist and his clients, usually governmental administrators or legislators, is not difficult because it requires no translation from technical to lay language. On the other hand, the sophistication and progress of a discipline vary in direct ratio to its technicality, and the virtue here of communicability appears as the obverse of a greater fault.

It is not difficult to see that political research is wanting in its substantive knowledge and in the formulation of the insights it does have. To what is this lack of progress due? One is inclined to reply, with perhaps some exaggeration: The American political scientist is born free but is everywhere in chains, tied to a hyperfactual past.[14] The lack of more reliable knowledge flows directly from an immoderate neglect of general theory.

We cannot, to be sure, place on this neglect the sole blame for the slow advance of political science toward reliable knowledge and understanding of political life. We could explain its slow pace in a number of different ways, each of which would throw some quantum of light on the matter. It can be argued that we live in an age of action rather than of contemplation and as a result all the social sciences must suffer. They are doomed to draw on the store of ideas and methods inherited from the recent past rather than to make contributions of their own. This explanation has a core of truth. In a world of turmoil, men are compelled to seek a solution for their immediate problems on the basis of the available inventory of ideas. The atmosphere for leisurely and exacting research into fundamentals is missing.

A small but insistent part of recent thinking in political science places the blame for the latter's slow development on the absence of serious attention to methods of research. The term "method" has always been a slippery concept laden with a varied store of meanings. In each of its numerous senses, shortcomings in method do contribute to some glaring deficiencies in research, although I shall urge that today these weaknesses are secondary when compared with the absence of a theoretical orientation.

We might attribute part of the cause for the inching pace of political research to the relative lack of concern for questions of methodology, the logic behind the scientific procedures which political scientists often say they are using. Such questions of logic are as relevant to political science as they are to all the social sciences and, for that matter, as they are to all the biological and physical sciences as well. Indeed, methodology is of particular importance for political science. The latter is the last of all the social sciences in the United States to feel the influence of rigorous scientific procedures. Since it is the last, it has been subjected to scientific treatment at the very time that the use of scientific method for an understanding of social problems is coming under renewed severe attack. The result is that there is a tendency for political science to become the battleground where the advocates and opponents of the use of scientific procedures fight out their issues.

Although methodology has a special importance in the catalogue of problems of method in political science, it is only one of the many causes to which the present underdeveloped state of political research has been attributed. We might correctly deal at some length with matters of technique.

American political research is still quite unsophisticated in this respect.[15] It still tends to collect and relate data in a casual, uninstructed way. The repertoire of techniques for controlled observation, such as the varieties of highly developed forms of interview and objective participation, the correlation of data, experimentation, and the testing of theories, so familiar to other social sciences, still finds only an irregular, almost accidental, place in the curriculum of students of politics.[16]

The absence of special concern for techniques has had the secondary result of keeping the research student from intimate contact with his material. Relatively few political scientists have the opportunity to participate extensively in high-level politics at the national and state capitols; a slightly broader group eddies about these scholars.[17] For the vast bulk of the profession this is manifestly impossible. But for this group it is often forgotten that a broad scope for direct field research of equal, if not overriding, importance exists in local politics. In their early training political scientists are rarely impressed with the need to make personal observations in the field according to acceptable standards for the collection of data. One could readily trace the damaging effects of this lack of intimate knowledge about political activity on the products of research.

It is possible to explain shortcomings in subject matter, and even in method, as the extravagant results of professional insensitivity to change. Fundamentally such deficiencies have their origin in the late nineteenth century. In the light of the stage of development of political science and of social science in general in that century, the problems selected for investigation and the procedures of research had their historic explanation and justification. Their continuation today, however, reflects the prestige that an ancestral way of life has for contemporary political science. Essentially political science today is traditionalist. Where a discipline develops a professional character, its attitudes and premises of research frequently strike deep roots. Its professionalism shelters its members from the vitalizing influence of the community as a whole. Even new recruits to the field who have by their own efforts sought training in the advanced techniques of the other social sciences are normally discouraged by the thick crust of tradition from transferring their knowledge to the study of political life. As a discipline political science has tolerated innovation; it has not encouraged it. The result is that inadequate procedures or formulations of substantive questions, once founded in the profession, have continued in spite of their manifest shortcomings, simply because the lore that has been bequeathed by teacher to student receives the protection of professional sanctity.

The traditions of a discipline as congealed in a professional outlook, however, can explain only the closest institutional source of current dominant conceptions of research in political science. Other social sciences are exposed to the same force and yet have not been victimized to the same extent. There is a deeper social reason for the failure of political science to transcend its limitations. It lies in the proximity of political research to the social forces that determine social policy. The findings of psychology, sociology, or economics, for instance, are less intimately connected with revealing the actual locus of power in the community or the channels whereby existing power formations struggle to influence social policy. However inadequate its success in this respect, political science is reaching toward an understanding of the very things that men consider most vital: their differences over what I describe as the authoritative allocation of values. Entrenched power groups in society, those who have a firm hold on a particular pattern of distribution of social goods, material and spiritual, have a special reason to look askance at this probing into the nature and source of their social positions and activities. They are prone to stimulate research of a kind that does not inquire into the fundamentals of the existing arrangement of things.[18] In varying degrees this is necessarily true of any society. History has yet to show us empowered groups who welcomed investigation into the roots and distribution of their strength. Such knowledge is at least discomforting, if not inherently dangerous; the underlying unifying myth concerning the location of power is seldom borne out by the facts.

It would be a mistake, of course, to insist that there is a direct and invariant causal relation here between the pace and depth of political research and its potential danger to those who actually possess social power. Political research has obviously remained neither static nor stagnant. The only point here is that the institutional matrix within which this research must be conducted has shaped and directed the growth of political science as a field more than it has the other social sciences. By the very nature of its research interests, political science is in a particularly exposed position, hence its virtual extinction in dictatorial countries. I am suggesting that elsewhere its proximity to sensitive areas of political power has helped to keep it close to the level of achievement attained at the beginning of the twentieth century, when it began to feel its first strength as an independent field for empirical research.

Many more reasons could be offered to explain the present state of political research. As I suggested at the outset, however, one stands out for its primary importance: the absence of a theoretical orientation to provide the basis for the kind of understanding of their data that students of political life seek. A keen sense of where and how to look for the locus of power and its influence, a clear perspective on the fundamental problems of the logic behind scientific method, unambiguous terminology, the introduction of new techniques and a deep awareness of the need to seek out intimacy with observed phenomena, even the growth of a professional spirit that in research seeks to rise above the value premises of the political system that research students may approve as citizens—these must all add up to little in the absence of a conceptual framework or systematic theory to give meaning, coherence, and direction to ongoing research. To the lack of no other single factor can we trace such grave consequences for the present condition in political science.

REFERENCES

1. A. Haddow, *Political Science in American Colleges and Universities* (New York: Appleton-Century-Crofts, 1939).
2. W. Anderson, "Political Science Enters the Twentieth Century," in A. Haddow, *op. cit.*, chap. 14.
3. *Ibid.*
4. Report of the Committee for the Advancement of Teaching, American Political Science Association, *Goals for Political Science* (New York: Sloane, 1951), p. xiv.
5. "Physiology and Politics," presidential address to sixth annual meeting of American Political Science Association in *American Political Science Review*, 4 (1910), 1–16.
6. L. B. Sims, "Social Scientists in the Federal Services," *Public Policy* (1940), 280–296.
7. F. A. Ogg, *Research in the Humanistic and Social Sciences* (New York: Appleton-Century-Crofts, 1928), p. 17.
8. V. O. Key, *Politics, Parties, and Pressure Groups* (New York: T. Y. Crowell, 1945), pp. 4–5.
9. Cf. R. Redfield, "The Art of Social Science," *American Journal of Sociology*, 54 (1948), 181–90.
10. That we do know something, however, is the conclusion of R. W. Gerard, "The Biological Basis of Imagination," *Scientific Monthly*, 62 (1946), 477–500.
11. This has been a recurring complaint, reflected in a comment by W. W. Willoughby at the beginning of the century. "In these days . . . ," he wrote, "it is a reproach to any science that its essential terms should not have precise meanings; yet this is precisely the condition in which political science finds itself. . . ." "The Value of Political Philosophy," *Political Science Quarterly*, 15 (1900), 86.
12. See a recent preliminary attempt at clarifying this concept in H. Simon, D. Smithburg, and V. Thompson, *Public Administration* (New York: Knopf, 1950), p. 513.
13. H. Simon, *Administrative Behavior* (New York: The Free Press, 1957), chap. 2.
14. For suggestions along other lines see UNESCO, *Contemporary Political Science* (Paris: UNESCO, 1950), articles on American political science; American Political Science Association, Committee on Instruction, *The Teaching of Government* (New York: Macmillan, 1916); C. E. Merriam *et al.*, "Report of Committee on

Political Research," *American Political Science Review,* 17 (1923), 274–312; T. H. Reed, "Report of Committee on Policy of the American Political Science Association," *American Political Science Review,* 24 (1930), supplement; C. E. Merriam, *New Aspects of Politics* (Chicago: University of Chicago Press, 1925); P. Appleby, "Political Science: The Next Twenty-five Years," *American Political Science Review,* 44 (1950), 924–32; P. Herring, "Political Science in the Next Decade," *American Political Science Review,* 39 (1945), 757–66.

15. Cf. H. D. Lasswell, "Psychology and Political Science in the U.S.A.," in UNESCO, *Contemporary Political Science, op. cit.,* pp. 526–37.

16. See Report of the Committee for the Advancement of Teaching, A.P.S.A., *op. cit.,* pp. 266 *ff.* where the Committee recommends that "One of the ways to improve the effectiveness of budding political scientists is to provide a good course on the scope and methods of political science as an introduction to all graduate work."

17. J. P. Harris *et al.,* "The Relations of Political Scientists with Public Officials," *American Political Science Review,* 35 (1941), 333–43.

18. Compare a related criticism by Ratzenhofer, over half a century ago, quoted in A. W. Small, *General Sociology* (Chicago: University of Chicago Press, 1905), p. 319. Here Ratzenhofer accuses politics of being a pseudo-science, a conclusion with which the penetrating American sociologist A. W. Small undoubtedly agreed, because it "displayed decided reluctance to use the probe relentlessly in research within political conditions."

2: *The Impact on Political Science of the Revolution in the Behavioral Sciences*

DAVID B. TRUMAN

Some time ago, in the course of a conversation with a social psychologist whose friendship and counsel I value highly, I mentioned my assignment to discuss with you tonight "The Impact on Political Science of the Revolution in the Behavioral Sciences" and confessed to him some misgivings about the assumptions implied by the title. "Has there been any impact?" I asked. His reply was, "Has there been any revolution?" The more I thought about this lecture, the more persistently this conversation has come to mind, until I have concluded that these are not, in fact, flippant questions and that I was obliged to give them a central place in this discussion, even though they may not be adequately answered, or even answerable. What is the nature of this alleged revolution? What kinds of effects has it had, if any,

Reprinted from Brookings Lectures, 1955, *Research Frontiers in Politics and Government* (Washington, D.C.: The Brookings Institution, 1955), pp. 202–31, by permission of the author and the publisher. The first footnote of the original article, identifying the author, has been omitted.

on the work of political scientists and, since many critics, in the discipline as well as outside of it, assume that these should be or will be considerable, what are the major intellectual obstacles to such impact? Are there limits, as distinguished from resistances, to the application to political science of developments in the behavioral sciences? What is the nature of these limits?

The term "behavioral sciences" is one of recent currency, and its variable meanings may, without a word or two of explanation, cause some confusion. It is sometimes used as an equivalent for the social sciences, a loose usage that is probably inevitable as long as the term is fashionable and is thought to provide a key to foundation cash boxes. More narrowly, and perhaps more accurately, the phrase refers to those bodies of knowledge, in whatever academic department they may be found, that provide or aspire to provide "verified principles" of human behavior through the use of methods of inquiry similar to those of the natural sciences. In conventional university organization, such knowledge and such aspirations may be found in a variety of places, from schools of public health to departments of linguistics, but their incidence is normally greatest in departments of psychology, sociology, and anthropology, and the term most commonly serves as a shorthand expression for the concerns typical of these three fields. This restricted meaning is the one that I shall use.

DEVELOPMENTS IN THE BEHAVIORAL SCIENCES

Whether or not they merit glorifying by the word "revolution," the developments in the behavioral sciences in the past three decades have been numerous and impressive. These I can no more than characterize and illustrate; cataloguing and sifting the tremendous volume of work during this period is a task for which I have neither the time nor the required capacities. If, however, one were to start from an intellectual event such as the publication of the *Encyclopaedia of the Social Sciences,* the first volume of which appeared nearly a quarter of a century ago, and were to reflect on the alterations that a competent board of editors would feel called upon to make in a new edition, he would, I suspect, be impressed not only with the general rate of obsolescence in the area during these twenty-five years but even more with the shift in the center of gravity within the social sciences toward the behavioral sciences.

For present purposes it is appropriate to examine these developments under two headings: developments in the realm of research technique and those in the realm of expanded theory and verified propositions. The first of these is, significantly, far easier and less treacherous to evaluate than the second, partly because development of the tools of data collection and analysis has been rapid and unmistakable.

In Research Technique

The techniques of the sample survey can claim a place at the top of any list of such developments, not only because they constitute a basic instrument of social research in their own right, but also because their refinement has stimulated a series of achievements, primarily in the invention of ancillary techniques but also to some extent in the construction of explanatory theory. The roots of this technique are fairly old, indeed ancient if one traces them back to the unsystematic efforts of politicians and journalists to estimate the intentions of a mass electorate. The core of the skill, however, is the design and administration of the population sample, and this is comparatively modern. Stimulated by the commercial utility of even fairly crude estimates of intentions and susceptibilities of consumers, rudimentary techniques of population sampling became a commonplace device in the business world by the 1920's. The potentialities of population sampling for noncommercial, social, and political research, however, were not widely recognized until the 1930's. Partly as a means of promoting the acceptance of these techniques in market analysis and partly as an opportunity for testing them against the official results of elections, polling of samples of prospective voters developed in the middle of the 1930's. What began as a by-product extended into fairly continuous surveys of popular opinion on various issues of the day, until "Gallup poll" became a generic term familiar over the globe.

In the United States at the same time those responsible for developing and administering many of the emergency programs undertaken in depression and war by the federal government needed new kinds of population statistics. A gradual recognition that sample studies may hold advantages in speed, efficiency, and cost over a complete enumeration led the Bureau of the Census and other governmental agencies, building on established theories of sampling and on experience in such fields as the estimating of crop yields, to make rapid improvements in the reliability of population samples. The rapidity of this development is suggested by the fact that the case book, *Methods in Social Science,*[2] published in 1933, contains no analysis of a study involving the direct sampling of individuals in a population. The *Encyclopaedia of the Social Sciences* contains no article on sampling, and, although the essays on statistics and on probability refer to sampling in biometrics, economics, and crop estimating and comment briefly on samples drawn from registration records and from complete enumerations, they contain no discussion of samples drawn directly from the human population. Both the state of the art and the character of existing obstacles are suggested in the following comment in the essay on "statistical practice" in the *Encyclopaedia of the Social Sciences:* "It is so difficult to insure representativeness of the sample that in most inquiries relative to population complete enumeration is preferred."[3]

"Representativeness" was a problem in practical sampling rather than in general theory. Experience with the quota sample, on which opinion surveyors relied in the 1930's, and the development of probability sampling by the Bureau of the Census and the Bureau of Agricultural Economics in the early 1940's reduced this problem to manageable proportions.

Paralleling and, in part, flowing from the growth of skill in sampling, a number of techniques, both for the collection and for the analysis of data have been invented or significantly improved. Thus as the crudity of samples has been reduced, attention has been turned to the inadequacies in interviewing. The sources of unreliability have been explored and their bearing on the validity of results has been examined in systematic fashion, so that the dangers in this phase have been identified even though the means of controlling them have not been fully provided.[4]

At the same time, criticism and experimentation have contributed materially to increasing sophistication in the design of survey questions and questionnaires and in the substantive aspects of interviews generally. Drawing on and adapting experience in counseling and psychotherapy, the design and administration of questions have come a long way from the intuitive, rather hit-or-miss techniques used in early opinion and community surveys. The merits of the open-ended question as compared with the fixed-alternative or "poll-type" question and of the focused or "depth" interview have been explored and developed to the point where the investigator's range of choice among interviewing tools has markedly widened.[5]

The process of adaptation just referred to is one of considerable significance for the topic under discussion and is therefore deserving of some emphasis for its own sake. It is one, perhaps the major, example of a strong tendency on the part of the sample survey technicians and of others engaged in the collection of data from large numbers of people. Where devices for the study of individual psychological characteristics and behaviors, whether diagnostic or purely analytical, have been developed satisfactorily, and where they have appeared adaptable without major losses in efficiency to the study of large numbers of cases, as in the sample survey, adaptation has occurred rather quickly. One effect of this has been to reinforce preoccupation with the attitudes and behaviors of individuals. It has emphasized, almost to the point of excluding other sorts of objectives, preoccupation with arriving at what might be called the "people-who" type of statement; that is, people who reveal a certain psychological characteristic tend to perceive, understand, speak, or behave in such-and-such fashion. Propositions of this sort, of course, are not without value in many situations, but, for reasons that I shall attempt to explore in more detail somewhat later, they may have only limited significance for the problems with which the political scientist is characteristically concerned.[6]

In slightly different fashion the maturing of sample-survey methods has been stimulated by and has contributed to advances in techniques of measurement, notably the analysis of attitudes through the use of scales. The early work of Bogardus, Thurstone, and Likert was largely independent of the techniques of the sample survey. As the later devices have begun, however, to produce data of greater reliability, warranting the use of more precise techniques of analysis than the early polls justified and inviting more complicated sorts of inferences than they could support, the two research tendencies have come together. Significant steps have been taken, notably in the work of Guttman, Lazarsfeld, and others, to adapt and extend the earlier measurement devices, thereby stimulating significantly more penetrating analysis of survey data.[7] Similarly, the survey device has been extended to approximate some of the power and efficiency of experimentation through the use of the so-called panel technique. By successive re-interviews of a population sample—the panel—it is possible to get at changes, and at some of the causes of changes, in attitudes and behavior.

The past two decades have also seen a considerable development and extension of experimentation, both in the controlled laboratory setting and in the natural situation. This has taken various forms. Among them are the numerous techniques for observing, recording, and analyzing behavior in small groups which, especially since the work of Elton Mayo and Kurt Lewin, have become the identifying equipment for specialists in the new "field" of group dynamics. Among these, reference should also be made to the techniques collectively known as sociometry, devised by J. L. Moreno for the analysis of interaction and influence structure in small groups. These and related developments, whether employed in the laboratory or in the "field," not only have contributed a considerable body of information on face-to-face groups of various sorts but also have provided stimulus to greater sophistication in observational field work generally.[8]

Finally, it may be appropriate to mention the elaboration and expansion of the techniques for analyzing communications content. Although their beginnings run back considerably more than twenty-five years, the skills of the content analyst, especially with respect to the devices for systematic classification and for quantitative analysis, have received a marked degree of extension and refinement within the past two decades.[9]

This cursory and necessarily superficial glance at some recent developments in the behavioral sciences is sufficient at least to suggest that within the realm of technique it is reasonable to speak of major developments. One may legitimately think of this as a technological revolution, even if one concludes that, unlike other such changes, its consequences are limited.

In Theory

When one turns to the realm of theory, especially theory resting on some measure of empirical verification, the task of evaluation becomes considerably more formidable. Not only are theories in the behavioral sciences numerous, but the possible implications of these formulations for the work of the political scientist have scarcely been explored. Any comment on this point, therefore, is likely to be superficial and subject to serious challenge.

At the risk of indulging in severe oversimplification, I should like to venture the observation that in the realm of theory the behavioral sciences have produced two quite different bodies of propositions, one rather narrowly concerned with individual behavior or with action in small, face-to-face groups and the other aimed at an inclusive explanation of a wide range of action not specifically relevant to any particular institutional context. Although it is doubtful that in either of these there is much in the way of revolutionary content, both have some value for the student of political processes and institutions. At the same time, however, neither more than approaches a solution to the most troublesome problems in such study. The difficulty of estimating the existing or the probable impact of behavioral science theory on political science lies precisely in the gap between these two statements. Behavioral science theory has implications of value to the student of politics, but it goes no more than part of the way toward the solution of his intellectual problems.

So sweeping a characterization cannot, certainly within the limits of a single lecture, be proved, but it clearly calls at least for illustration and for argument. I should assert that a sizable fraction of behavioral science theory, whether in psychology, sociology, or anthropology, is noninstitutional. That is, it is principally concerned with explaining the effects of a given institutional pattern on the behavior of an individual or an aggregate of individuals and not with explaining or even describing the operation of the institution itself. Thus, of course, all or almost all of psychology is individual. The preoccupations of psychology are with categories and processes of individual behavior—learning, conditioning, motivation, perception, discrimination, and so on. Again, despite the existence of competing doctrines, a major preoccupation remains the characteristics and development of individual personality under the influence of physiological and, more recently, social factors.

The growth of social psychology has increased the number and kinds of factors considered in the whole gamut of psychological analysis, but it has not changed the emphasis. Concerned with the behavior of men in groups, the social psychologist is nevertheless characteristically interested in the effects of group environments on the behavior of individuals, in the individual psychology of interpersonal influence.[10]

For understandable reasons the environments most closely studied by the social psychologist have been those of small, face-to-face groups, whether in experimental or natural situations—family, club, classroom, gang, clique, and neighborhood. These groupings are more amenable to the requirements of scientific procedure than are more inclusive formations. It seems probable, moreover, that, if one is concerned principally with effects on individual behavior, such groups are primary, in the sense of degree of importance, and therefore peculiarly basic to the discipline.

Not all concerns with the small group have been exclusively psychological, of course. As the curiosities and theories of the investigator become more characteristically sociological, they are less concerned with effects on individuals than with the structure of groups and with the effects on group performance resulting from differences in intragroup communication, from variations in the performance of specialized roles within the group, and from variations in the tasks undertaken by it.

This borderland of psychology, sociology, and anthropology, which has come to be known most commonly as group dynamics, has produced a respectable body of theory, both basic and applied, notably on the subject of leadership.[11] Its preoccupations, however, are only slightly less microcosmic than those of the psychologist and are only slightly less non-institutional. Much this same point was made by Herbert Simon in his lecture in this series, and some of the nonpolitical scientists working in the area, particularly those whose investigations have been conducted in the "field" rather than in the laboratory, have become aware of it. As one of the "field" researchers has put it, ". . . we simply cannot extrapolate conclusions from the small group studies when we are dealing with groups in large organizations."[12] Or, in the words of a theorist and practitioner in applied anthropology, "The evidence . . . seems to indicate that building theory upon research concentration on the small group may be mistaken, however experimentally justifiable as an object of research the small group may be. The individual behavior that psychology seeks to explain seems to be less a property of groups or the group in particular than one of processes of social interaction in general, inclusive of both large and small groups."[13] If, as he goes on to argue, changes in basic social relationships, in individual and collective attitudes, and in individual behavior tend to occur *in that order,* then a theory that starts from the latter end of the sequence has limited utility for the student of larger institutional complexes, and its limited uses, as I shall point out somewhat later, involve serious hazards.

Although the sociological and anthropological concern with small groups, which considerably antedates the more psychologically oriented research in group dynamics, has been more likely to place the group in a larger institutional context and to investigate changes stemming from such contexts, its focus has remained the small unit. The broadest reach in empirical terms within these fields, moreover, has been the small city or community, although perhaps exception should be made of some kinds of broad, aggregative research concerned with social class and demography. The formulation of theory of a more inclusive sweep has not been, strictly speaking, the objective or the product of the efforts of the behavioral scientist. That function has been left to the more historically and philosophically inclined sociologist or anthropologist, concerned with reflections about the state of society, in the tradition of Max Weber and Mannheim, or to speculative synthesizing like that of Talcott Parsons.

By way of preliminary summary, the developments in the behavioral sciences over the past quarter century, thus cursorily and perhaps somewhat unfairly reviewed, appear a good deal more revolutionary in the realm of technique than in that of validated and expanded theory. Both the characteristic techniques, moreover, and the tested propositions, of which the number is considerable, typically have been microcosmic. Both have concentrated on the individual or on the restricted group to the virtual exclusion of larger organizations and more inclusive institutions.

Though this concentration has occurred, one should not assume that in either respect the behavioral sciences have no relevance for the political scientist. But it should not be astonishing that their area of greatest impact to date has been in connection with the study of voting behavior, the most individualized, in a sense most uncomplicated, and perhaps least important element in the political process. The theory that has emerged, largely through the use of the sample survey technique, is exclusively a social psychological theory of electoral choice, with only the barest suggestions of implications for other features of the electoral or political process.

A further word should be said, however, concerning theoretical developments in behavioral science. Whatever the limits on its scope and on its applicability to the problems of the political scientist, theory in the behavioral sciences has become far more completely fused with empirical research and theorizing has become more self-consciously central to the concerns of investigators than was the case shortly after

World War I. One has the distinct impression that the volume of taxonomic description of concrete phenomena has declined and that there has occurred an increased and general commitment to the discovery of uniformities, to the use of observation for the verification of hypotheses, and to the search for empirically supported generalizations.

The traces of this can be seen in several areas not far from the concerns of the political scientist. As Herbert Simon has pointed out, significant beginnings have been made on an organizational theory, although it cannot yet help us much in dealing with large and complicated structures. From various sources in the behavioral sciences the suggestive concept of role has been developed, through which a number of significant propositions of potentially broad relevance have been formulated. Some preliminary elements of a theory of communications are beginning to appear. Along somewhat different lines, there has been an increasing interest in the creation and exploitation of formal models, of which the theory of games, discussed in Richard Snyder's recent lecture, is a major example. Whatever one may think of the utility of any such models, and in my opinion skepticism is in order, experimenting with them at least represents a serious theoretical preoccupation. Much the same thing may be said of the efforts of Parsons and his associates to develop a general theory of action. This inclusive effort at a high level of abstraction admittedly seems to promise to be valid immediately only for relatively simple features of a social system. Whether or not one shares the implied faith that the treatment of more complex characteristics is almost within reach, one must acknowledge that this effort, along with less ambitious theoretical endeavors, nevertheless represents a considerable degree of ferment—a renewed commitment to theory and to the discovery and statement of behavioral uniformities.

Such ferment, I should like to suggest, such renewed commitment, may alone have more significant impact on the work of the political scientist than the content of the theories, the substantive material of the validated propositions, or the innovations in technique, important though these may be.

CONVENTIONAL RESEARCH IN POLITICAL SCIENCE

Turning more directly to the impact side of the topic, it is perhaps appropriate to look for a moment at the character of the traditional research concerns of American political science. These have been decidedly heterogeneous over the field as a whole, from the conventional textual analysis of political philosophy to the latest study of legislative policy making. The most common element in research in political science, one can fairly say, has been institutional description. This does not adequately cover, perhaps, much of the familiar concern with the assessment and prescription of public policy, more than a segment of the historico-legal research in public law, nor more than a minor fraction of the writing of current history, which has given much of political science the quality of heavy-handed periodical journalism. Yet despite this incompleteness, one can safely assert that the description of governmental and paragovernmental institutions has been and continues to be our characteristic preoccupation as a profession.

Criticisms of this focus from various standpoints are not new. They can be seen as early as the first years of this century in the writings of Graham Wallas and in the strictures of Arthur F. Bentley. What was known for a time during the 1920's and 1930's as the "Chicago school" of political science, gathered around the stimulating person of the late Charles E. Merriam, represented a fairly explicit revolt against the established tradition. But with the achievements, especially the technical innovations, in recent years in the behavioral sciences—perhaps in part because of their enhanced popular prestige—the volume of such criticism seems to have increased—in books, in papers at annual meetings, in the professional journals, and, perhaps most conspicuously, in the shoptalk of many younger members of the profession.

The latter-day rebels have mostly rallied around the banner of "political behavior" to do battle with the "institutionalists." Like most embattled revolutionists, many of them have unwisely and impetuously consigned to oblivion all the works of their predecessors. This is unfortunate not only because it does injustice and betrays a lack of discrimination, but more seriously because it tends unnecessarily to widen the gulf between the two groups and to obscure the precise points at issue and thereby to postpone the discovery of solutions.

Despite appearances to the contrary, there are basic similarities in the assumptions and objectives, albeit usually implicit, of the "institutionalists" and their opponents. The latter may argue that they alone are committed to the discovery and statement of regularities in the political process. Or they may assert that they alone hold the objective of predictability. Neither of these alleged monopolies is genuine, however. There are some differences along these lines, but one should not forget that to describe a court, a legislature, or a government agency, in however formal terms, is to assume that there is regularity in political processes that can be stated. Likewise, to do any of these things or to analyze a line of court cases or the pronouncements of a legislative committee is usually to assume, although perhaps largely implicitly, the persistence of such patterns under appropriate conditions and to accept the possibility, and even to a degree the responsibility, of prediction.

Nor am I persuaded that the cleavage within political science lies between description and something else, and I note that in assertions of this sort the "something else" is often vaguely stated or involves a false opposition. For instance, in the report of one of five university surveys in the behavioral sciences conducted during 1954, the following passage occurs: "Political Science has been giving increasingly serious attention to the behavioral approach to political research problems, moving toward the empirical *investigation of specific propositions* about political behavior at the same time that it is continuing with the *institutional-descriptive* type of research."[14] There is surely nothing necessarily nondescriptive or even noninstitutional about a proposition concerning the political process. Virtually all propositions about political behavior are, and for some time are likely to remain, descriptive. In fact, the same thing is true of most of the established propositions in the behavioral sciences. Only their most zealous defender would, I suspect, deny that the dynamic or causal, as distinguished from the descriptive, element in most of the latter is comparatively small. The point at which a statistically significant correlation becomes less descriptive and more nearly explanatory is not easily identified.

NEW TENDENCIES IN POLITICAL SCIENCE

I have gone into these distinctions, which I believe erroneous, because I am certain that there are accurate ones to be drawn, genuine differences in tendency within the field that have become the more marked through the impact of experiences and inventions in the behavioral sciences. If these divergences do not lie with broad, if implicit, assumptions about regularity and predictability or with degrees of concern for description, what are their bases? I should like to deal briefly with four of these in what seems to me the order of their importance: first, the difference in the nature of the commitment to discovering regularities; second, differences in the approach to institutions; third, differences in data; and fourth, differences in technique.

Though both groupings in political science assume the

existence and discoverability of regularities in political behavior, for the "institutionalist" this assumption is usually
implicit, a logical inference from his conduct rather than a
consciously asserted objective. A more explicit pursuit of
regularities has several consequences, of which I shall refer
to two.

In the first place, the researcher is prepared to find similarities of pattern between or among formal institutions rather
than merely within them. In other words, he expects to be
able to abstract from the concrete phenomena of institutional
behavior and to identify the occurrence of classes or categories of phenomena and, thereby, to be able to generalize
over a wider range of concretely divergent or unique situations or relationships. This is an unfamiliar objective only
in degree. For example, political scientists, along with other
social scientists and laymen as well, have long assumed that
certain regularities of behavior and situation are referred to
by the term "political leadership," or even just "leadership,"
whether one is looking at a ward boss, a Speaker of the
United States House of Representatives, or a President of
the United States. The self-conscious pursuit of this sort of
intellectual objective is, of course, not an end in itself, fas-
cinating though it may be, but, like abstract thinking in
whatever form, it is a means of simplifying and ordering
experience and observation so that the mind is confronted
by a finite number of *types* of problems and challenges
rather than by a bewilderingly infinite number of these. It is
a long step forward in any field to identify such categories.

A more explicit pursuit of regularities, in the second place,
is, perhaps somewhat paradoxically, likely to lead to a greater
awareness of the variations in the *conditions* under which
institutional or other patterns occur and to a search for regularities in those conditions. An unself-conscious or merely
incidental interest in behavioral uniformities produces both
a preoccupation with the unique in institutional form and
operation and a curious willingness to accept the superficial

regularities suggested by a name or nominally prescribed by similar legal arrangements. We would all agree that the operative structure and the sociopolitical functions constituting two political parties or two legislatures are not necessarily the same even though conventionally they are referred to by the same term or despite the fact that they appear to operate under similar rules or laws. And we would accept the proposition that any one such institution is not necessarily structurally or functionally the same at two points in time although it may bear the same name and although its formal features remain unchanged. Yet characteristically our literature both concedes this point and persists in talking about *the* political party or *the* legislature, avoiding the issue of regularity of pattern either by minute description of a single institution in a limited span of time or by proceeding as if differences in time and space did not exist or were of no real consequence. An explicit dedication to the search for uniformities, characteristic of work in the behavioral sciences, makes either of these alternatives less readily available.

As the preceding remarks suggest, a second difference in the tendencies within the field is in the approach to political institutions, the example of the behavioral sciences encouraging hesitation to take them at their formal or face value, even when the research objective is no more than description. Avoidance of this tendency does not mean merely a skepticism about the descriptive validity of formal arrangements, though this may be in psychological terms a necessary precondition to the effort I refer to. It means, rather, a search for conceptual tools, analytical categories if you will, that are not defined by or equivalent to formal institutional units or subunits. One is not escaping from the restrictive influence of formalities if, in analyzing the policy-forming process, he is obliged to talk in terms of *the* political party or *the* legislature, for in so doing he inescapably begs a portion of the question he is attempting to answer.

What is required in the circumstances is what I like to

think of as a "tracer element," or a series of them, through the examination of which one can describe consistent patterns of interaction, including institutional ones and including the relevance for such patterns of the formal features of the institutions. Such was and, in my opinion, is the promise of the notion of group as it was introduced to American political science by Arthur F. Bentley. Although it has had considerable beneficial influence, however, including the early work on legislative voting blocs, it has been so narrowly viewed as pressure group that it has often merely added another element of formality rather than provided a new means of ordering the data of behavior in and around governmental institutions.

The current search for unconventionalized categories is reflected in a variety of ways in contemporary political science. It accounts, I suspect, for much of the current fascination with the analysis of voting behavior, where the sample survey technique in combination with various sociopsychological categories permits the development of descriptive propositions and even some significant hypotheses concerning the dynamics of the voting choice and the beginnings of some perceptual definitions of institutions such as political parties.[15] It clearly underlies the recent stirrings in the area of the comparative analysis of governments, where it has become apparent to many that conventional formal categories like "executive," "legislature," "political party," and "bureaucracy" are not in fact comparable because they have no consistent meaning independent of political and cultural boundaries, a limitation that is not adequately corrected by the addition of economic and social data to the range of phenomena taken into consideration.[16] It is indicated in Gabriel Almond's suggestive notions concerning specialized structures and functions affecting the formation of foreign policy.[17] Karl Deutsch's interesting attempt to deal with nationalism in terms of a theory of communication[18] and the efforts of Richard C. Snyder and his associates to work out categories for the analysis of decision-making,[19] whatever their ultimate usefulness may prove to be, are significant symptoms of the same sort of striving. Finally, the search in a few bold cases has taken the form of an attempt to develop formal models or theories of an explicitly political sort, relating types of processes and relationships not "given" in the conventionalized data into sets of schemes in terms of which political action may be explained and possibly predicted. An example here is the cross-disciplinary theorizing of Robert Dahl and Charles Lindblom, which was partially summarized in the former's lecture in this series.[20]

All of these efforts—and many more would have to be included in an adequately representative list—indicate even in their diversity a common response to the need for concepts and sets of concepts in terms of which governmental processes and structures may be analyzed without the limiting assumptions imposed by conventional institutional categories.

The two divergences from established patterns of political science research so far discussed, namely, the more explicit commitment to regularities and the search for new analytical categories, encourages, though they do not require, the two others—differences in data and differences in techniques. Though many comments would imply that these last two are the more important of the four, a tendency of which I shall have more to say shortly, they seem to me decidedly secondary. In the first place, these tendencies may call for a broadening and enriching of the existing sources of evidence and a shift of emphasis toward the solicited responses of actors on the political scene and toward observing a wide range of activities not recorded in the conventional documentary sources, but they do not necessarily imply a rejection of the testimony stored on library shelves. In the second place, though there is a certain fascination in discovering, for example, the kinds of data that can be plowed up by the sample survey and though new conceptions of data demand

appropriate devices for collecting them and generally a
greater degree of self-consciousness about techniques, this
alone provides no assurance of increased validity. In studies
of political behavior there is and will continue to be a trend
toward the use of quantification, but there is no magic in
numbers unguided by relevant theory and well-articulated
hypotheses. Technical developments in the behavioral sciences, perhaps especially skills involved in the conduct and
analysis of interviews, are part of the recent stimulus to self-
criticism in political science, and an awareness of them may
distinguish the student of political behavior from his more
conventional colleagues, but it is technique in the service of
formulated theory whose impact promises to be most significant in the long run.

LIMITATIONS ON THE APPLICATION OF
THE BEHAVIORAL SCIENCES

If we can agree on the nature of the developments in the behavioral sciences, here roughly outlined, and on the evidence
that these have had some impact on the work of political
scientists, it is important to emphasize the point that to es-
pouse the extension of the latter tendency is not equivalent
to advocating simply the projection or importation of the
behavioral sciences into the sphere of political science. Although the general task of both is to develop empirically
testable theory and the means of validating it, and although
the student of political behavior can learn much from the
behavioral scientist, his particular task is peculiar, if not
unique. If my earlier analysis of the divergencies within political science is valid, then the two tendencies have more in
common substantively than either has with the behavioral
sciences, for both are engaged in the effort, each in its own
way, to analyze and explain the institutions and processes of
government. Whatever new roads to this objective may be

laid out, the destination remains the same. Much though we may learn from the experience of the behavioral sciences, the task of adapting that experience to our own needs remains exceedingly difficult, and admiring the neighbor's clearing fells no trees in one's own woodlot.

The Emphasis on Institutions

We are still committed to the study of a particular set of institutions, and this commitment carries with it some implications that may be worth fairly close examination. In the first place, I am not disposed seriously to quarrel with what I understand as the meaning of an observation, in the volume of essays entitled *Toward a General Theory of Action*, in which the authors suggest, "If the empirical focus of political science is to remain on the phenomena of government, it will not as a discipline be able to attain a sharpness of theoretical focus comparable to that of economics. It is more likely to draw from a much wider range of the components of the general theory of action and to find its distinctiveness in the way it combines these components in relation to its special empirical interests, rather than in the technical elaboration of a narrow and sharply focused segment of the theory of action, as is the case with economics."[21] A general theory of the sort attempted in that provocative volume necessarily abstracts from the peculiarities of particular institutional complexes, including government, and to attempt to introduce into such a theoretical structure the specialized factors associated with any specific institution is almost certain to involve theorizing efforts as great as those expended on the original. One would not expect to find clear contradictions between a theory of political behavior and an accepted general action theory, but one equally should not expect to derive directly from the latter a set of propositions adequately descriptive of a particular institutional system such as government.

Secondly, as a consequence of the institutional specialization that is inevitably characteristic of political science, it follows that the direct relationship between the behavioral sciences and political science is roughly that between "basic" and "applied" research. Narrowly defined, the objective of the behavioral sciences is the statement of "verified principles" of human behavior, taking account, perhaps, of general types of influencing conditions but without reference to any specific institutional context. The general outlook and even many of the methods of research in political behavior may be, in fact should be, consistent with this sort of objective, but their reference is necessarily to a particular order of institutional arrangements, the governmental. A behavioral scientist may from time to time, as many in fact do, make use of political data and governmental institutions, but his purpose as a behavioral scientist is not to arrive at propositions about government.

The political scientist, on the other hand, can and should make use of accepted hypotheses and promising models developed in the behavioral sciences, but he must always introduce into these the complicating parameters characteristic of the particular institutional complex with which he is concerned. In this sense, even his "basic" research, if he is performing his accepted job, is "applied" research from the standpoint of the behavioral sciences. This is no simple or lowly task; it is, in fact, so difficult, at least at present, that the political scientist can take the models and hypotheses of behavioral science merely as suggestions rather than as guides. The notion that a general science of human behavior can be developed as a source of guiding models for the analysis of behavior in particular contexts is a matter of faith, not of fact. The relationship of behavioral science to political research, therefore, involves no such simple operations as allowing for friction and wind resistance in adapting a physical model to an engineering situation.

There are and will continue to be various levels of research in political science, the more basic abstracting from a greater variety of temporal and spatial particularities, but the continuing institutional focus of political science remains at all levels the defining, and in a sense limiting, factor. This point, it seems to me, is a fundamental one. It is often ignored by behavioral scientists themselves, as when they leap, with irresponsible—one is tempted to say fraudulent—disregard for inconvenient and complicating problems—from a set of observations about child-rearing practices to the most bewilderingly complex concerns of men and nations. I emphasize it, however, not for this reason, but for three others of more importance for political science. Unless the point is kept clearly in mind, it seems to me, the political scientist runs the dangers, first, of failing to be what he pretends to be, a student of political institutions, second, of becoming ensnared in futile and myopic preoccupations with technique, and third, of misusing the materials of behavioral science. I should like to look briefly at each of these.

I have earlier suggested that the center of gravity in the behavioral sciences is individual or at least noninstitutional in character. This implies that an uncritical adoption of the methods and propositions of behavioral science involves taking over the questions and problems—and limitations—of the latter and that one who does so risks ceasing to be a political scientist. Thus, recurrently it is suggested that the salvation of political science lies in concentrating on the dynamic psychology of individuals, in analyzing individual actors in depth. Without denying the possible general relevance of such investigations, I should still not see how they permit one to move from the clinic to the institutional context, not alone as a practical matter but as one of logic. The political scientist cares little, for example, about what a judge does to the Supreme Court—unless he is the instrument of a major redirection of its activities—and still less about the effect on him of membership on the Court. He cares rather about the role of the Court in the society, its functioning in the process of societal adjustment and in the allocation of values. This involves, perhaps, the analysis of individual behavior, but the generalizations sought are about the institution, not about the individual actor.[22] In this connection I might cite an observation by two social psychologists, arguing a very similar point some years ago with critics in that field: "If we consider the effects of a man's behavior upon his fellows it is often not necessary to know his personality. His action may be deeply interiorized within him, or it may not be at all characteristic of him. But its effect upon his fellows may be the same."[23] If our target is to generalize about the characteristic patterns of an institution and the alterations therein, the underlying personality drives of individual participants are likely to be at most of peripheral importance.

Techniques Unrelated to Political Science

The second danger I wish to identify is the closely related one of treating technique as an end in itself, with little or no reference to the questions and problems of central importance in the discipline. The social sciences generally seem peculiarly liable to internecine, sectarian controversies over technique and method. Typical is the struggle between the partisans of the case study and the supporters of quantification, which has moved through one field after another like an epidemic of measles through a large family. The outcome, in some instances, happily has been a gradual acceptance of the uses and limitations of each in tackling specified types of problems. In others, however, and in a good many cases where no actual clash occurs, the result is for each camp to go happily about refining and sharpening its technique and promoting it as the only way to intellectual salvation.

A related phenomenon is the technical fad, in which a new device is taken up so widely that a researcher feels deficient if his study does not contain an application of the latest gadget, whether or not it is relevant to his substantive problem. At its lowest level this takes the form of a passion to punch and tabulate IBM cards without defining the questions on which the results are supposed to bear. At a more sophisticated level it involves defining the problem at hand in terms of a favorite technique rather than insisting that the problem set the technique. To a degree these tendencies are understandable and inevitable, and I certainly imply no censure of the specialist who devotes his energies to the perfecting of a technique in the faith that eventually it will prove of major usefulness. But the follower or borrower, especially from another field, is almost literally wasting his substance if he permits himself to expend his energies on the application of a technique without reference to its bearing on his most pressing problems of description and analysis. It would be a pity if political science were to adopt the position of the inebriated gentleman who, having lost his watch in a dark alley while making his way home in the small hours of the night, insisted on searching for it near the lamp post on the main street because there was more light there.

Misuse of Materials

Finally, the danger of misusing the materials of behavioral science presents itself when the political scientist, deliberately attempting to apply the findings of psychology or sociology, fails adequately to take into account the factors peculiar to the institution that he is studying. This pitfall in the path of an entirely commendable eclecticism is encountered most commonly in moving from the restricted situation, particularly that of the laboratory, into the complex realities of the political scene. We can note with sober caution the remark of Robert Sears, in a slightly different connection, that "An appallingly small number of the relationships that have been discovered in social psychology can be generalized beyond the immediate situation in which the studies were made."[24]

Thus if one is impressed with the suggestive findings in

group dynamics, most of which are built on observations in experimental situations or in limited natural contexts, he can use these only by a process of reasoning by analogy, with all its hazards, or by the more difficult process of introducing into the simple model of the face-to-face group the complicating parameters of the larger institutional setting, or by a combination of the two. One may be quite warranted, for example, in assuming that *in some respects* a legislative committee is *like* a problem-solving group set up for experimental purposes. But one cannot assume either that they are alike in all relevant respects or that these observed or attributed similarities are more significant than their differences in an explanation of their operation. Proceeding cautiously from minimal assumptions of similarity, one may in his speculative planning begin to take account of the possibility that the function of a committee may be to perpetuate disagreement, rather than to produce viable solutions, of the effects on the activities of a committee deriving from its place in the legislative structure, of the significance of the relations of members with leadership elements such as the presidency and with extragovernmental units like constituency parties and interest groups, of the political aspirations and anxieties of the committee members, and so on.

One thus tends to emerge with a theory of legislative committees bearing at most only a root resemblance to the laboratory-based theory of the face-to-face group. By introducing parameters such as these into his group model, moreover, the political scientist may so complicate the latter that the analytical techniques appropriate to the simpler situation may be useless for him. Yet he has no genuine alternative, as I see it, if he wishes to make legitimate use of the suggestive propositions of the behavioral scientist. Direct analogy is at best superficial and at worst seriously misleading. And if the introduction of complicating parameters makes a theoretical model unmanageable, the latter is the element that is expendable.

Parenthically, it is worth noting that the sort of problem I have referred to here is not encountered solely in the relations between political science and the behavioral sciences. It was a focus of the 1954 Social Science Research Council summer seminar on field and laboratory studies in social psychology as a problem *within* that field. A statement by the group, noting that ". . . theoretical statements emerging from field studies seem to be generally at a lower level of abstraction than those from laboratory experiments and likely to be more closely connected with specific empirical events," points out that ". . . this different orientation toward theory results in noncorrespondence between field and laboratory findings."[25]

CONCLUSION

The position I have attempted to develop can be roughly summarized as follows. The developments in the behavioral sciences over the past quarter-century have been more striking in the realm of technique than in that of validated and expanded theory. In both there has been a growing influence on the work and thought of political scientists. Though both types of impact are important, I should argue that the concern for empirically based theory, for the discovery and statement of behavioral uniformities, is the more fundamental. This influence has had the consequence of creating a divergence between what, for want of better terms, I have referred to as the "institutionalist" tendency in political science and the "political behavior" tendency. The differences between these two are genuine, lying in the character of their commitments to the discovery of uniformities, in their approach to political institutions, and to a lesser degree, in the types of data and technique with which they are concerned.

Genuine though they may be, however, these divergences may not be as great as they appear. Moreover, their real proportions and their implications may perhaps be better

understood if we give more explicit recognition to the obstacles in the way of adapting the techniques and particularly
the theories of the behavioral sciences, narrowly conceived,
to the problems that are the peculiar concern of the political
scientist. I would fully accept the proposition that the advance of our discipline lies in the acceptance of generaliza-
tion as its primary objective and of empirically testable theory
as its principal method; that advance will lose no speed from
a critical familiarity with both the techniques and the theories
of the behavioral sciences, but it has much to lose, in my
opinion, from an incautious attempt merely to project these
into the realm of governmental institutions.

This position is likely to be rejected or objected to by at
least two sets of critics. In the first place, those who do not
share my concern for the difficulties in the way of extending
into the study of political institutions the techniques and
theories of the behavioral sciences will view these statements
as defeatist if not treasonable. Those who regard optimisti-
cally the prospects of a general behavioral theory precisely
relevant to the realm of government and productive of hypothetical relationships subject to empirical test especially will
dismiss these arguments as parochial and shortsighted. To
these I can reply only that, given the complexity and the
crucial importance of governmental institutions in the societies with which we are most concerned, an empirically oriented but explicitly political theory seems to me the more
promising road to our mutual objective of predictability.

In the second place, my emphasis on theory and particularly on empirically testable theory may produce objections
from the "institutionalists" and from practitioners that pursuits of this sort will reduce the practical usefulness of the
political scientist without compensating gains. An adequate
reply to these would require more time than is presently
available, but it would include at least these propositions:
that there is nothing so practical as a well-developed and
testable theory; that the choice lies not between an approach

to such theory and no theory at all, but between an implicit and unexamined set of assumptions and an explicit theoretical effort; and, finally, that an implicit theory, though practically adequate in many circumstances, is likely to prove unsatisfactory in both practical and intellectual terms when dealing with a dynamic system subject to rapid and largely unplanned change.

On one point we can perhaps all agree; namely, that the entire social science enterprise will gain from a critical sensitivity to problems and developments in every corner of the vineyard and that all stand to lose when necessarily tentative intellectual positions are taken as gospel.

REFERENCES

1. See the source note to this chapter.
2. Stuart Rice, ed., *Methods in Social Science* (Chicago: University of Chicago Press, 1931).
3. Robert M. Woodbury, "Statistics: Statistical Practice," *Encyclopaedia of the Social Sciences,* vol. 14.
4. Herbert Hyman, *Interviewing in Social Research* (Chicago: University of Chicago Press, 1954).
5. *Cf.* C. R. Rogers, *Counseling and Psychotherapy* (Boston: Houghton Mifflin, 1942) and Robert K. Merton, *The Focused Interview* (New York: The Free Press, 1955).
6. *Cf.* Edward A. Shils, "Authoritarianism: Right and Left," in Richard Christie and Marie Jahoda, eds., *Studies in the Scope Method of "The Authoritarian Personality"* (New York: The Free Press, 1954), pp. 24–49 and David B. Truman, "Political Behavior and International Politics," *World Politics,* 3 (July 1951), 545–54.
7. See Samuel A. Stouffer and others, "Measurement and Prediction," *Studies in Social Psychology in World War II,* 4 (1950) and M. W. Riley, J. W. Riley, and J. Toby, *Scale Analysis* (1955).
8. See J. L. Moreno, *Who Shall Survive?* (1934) and Helen H. Jennings, *Leadership and Isolation* (New York: David McKay, 1943). See generally Marie Jahoda, Morton Deutsch, and Stuart W. Cook, *Research Methods in Social Relations* (New York: Holt, Rinehart & Winston, 1951); see also G. C. Homans, *The Human Group* (New York: Harcourt, Brace & World, 1950) and Dorwin Cartwright and Alvin Zander, eds., *Group Dynamics: Research and Theory* (New York: Harper & Row, 1953).

9. The best review of this technique is Bernard Berelson, *Content Analysis in Communications Research* (New York: The Free Press, 1952).

10. Note that the impressive psychological evidence regarding the consequences of segregation which was accepted by the U.S. Supreme Court (*Brown* v. *Topeka,* 347 U.S. 497, 1954) referred primarily and most directly to its effects upon individuals. See Kenneth B. Clark, "Desegregation: An Appraisal of the Evidence," *Journal of Social Issues,* 9:4 (1953).

11. For example, see Cartwright and Zander, *op. cit.,* Homans, *op. cit.,* and Harold S. Guetzkow, ed., *Groups, Leadership, and Men* (Pittsburgh: Carnegie Press, 1951; New York: Russell & Russell [reprint]).

12. W. F. Whyte, "Small Groups and Large Organizations," in J. H. Rohrer and M. Sherif, eds., *Social Psychology at the Crossroads* (New York: Harper & Row, 1951), p. 297.

13. C. M. Arensberg, "Behavior and Organization: Industrial Studies," in Rohrer and Sherif, *op. cit.,* p. 324.

14. Report of the Faculty Committee of the University of Michigan and Report of the Visiting Committee, *Survey of the Behavioral Sciences* (1954), p. 160. Italics added.

15. Angus Campbell, Gerald Gurin, and Warren E. Miller, *The Voter Decides* (New York: Harper & Row, 1954), chapts. 7 and 11.

16. Roy Macridis and others, "Research in Comparative Politics," *American Political Science Review,* 47 (September 1953), 641–75.

17. Gabriel A. Almond, *The American People and Foreign Policy* (New York: Praeger, 1950).

18. Karl W. Deutsch, *Nationalism and Social Communication* (Cambridge: MIT Press, 1953).

19. Richard C. Snyder, H. W. Bruck, and Burton Sapin, *Foreign Policy Decision-Making* (New York: The Free Press, 1962).

20. Robert A. Dahl and Charles E. Lindblom, *Politics, Economics and Welfare* (New York: Harper & Row, 1953).

21. Talcott Parsons and Edward A. Shils, eds., *Toward a General Theory of Action* (Cambridge: Harvard University Press, 1951), p. 29.

22. *Cf.* Richard C. Sheldon, "Some Observations on Theory in the Social Sciences," in Parsons and Shils, *op. cit.,* p. 40.

23. Daniel Katz and R. L. Schanck, *Social Psychology* (New York: John Wiley, 1938), p. 394.

24. Robert R. Sears, "Social Behavior and Personality Development," in Parsons and Shils, *op. cit.,* p. 466.

25. "Narrowing the Gap Between Field Studies and Laboratory Experiments in Social Psychology," *Social Science Research Council Items,* 8 (December 1954), 38.

3: The Behavioral Approach in Political Science: Epitaph for a Monument to a Successful Protest

ROBERT A. DAHL

Perhaps the most striking characteristic of the "behavioral approach" in political science is the ambiguity of the term itself, and of its synonym "political behavior." The behavioral approach, in fact, is rather like the Loch Ness monster: one can say with considerable confidence what it is not, but it is difficult to say what it *is*. Judging from newspaper reports that appear from time to time, particularly just before the summer tourist season, I judge that the monster of Loch Ness is not Moby Dick, nor my daughter's goldfish that disappeared down the drain some ten years ago, nor even a misplaced American eight heading for the Henley Regatta. In the same spirit, I judge that the behavioral approach is not that of the speculative philosopher, the historian, the legalist, or the moralist. What, then, is it? Indeed, does it actually exist?

Reprinted from *American Political Science Review*, 55 (December 1961), 763–72, by permission of the author and the publisher. The paper was first presented at the Fifth World Congress of the International Political Science Association, Paris, September 26, 1961.

I

Although I do not profess to know of the full history of the behavioral approach, a little investigation reveals that confusing and even contradictory interpretations have marked its appearance from the beginning. The first sightings in the roily waters of political science of the phenomenon variously called political behavioral approach, or behavioral(ist) research, evidently occurred in the 1920's. The term "political behavior," it seems, was used by American political scientists from the First World War onward.[1] The honor of first adopting the term as a book title seems to belong, however, not to a political scientist but to the American journalist Frank Kent, who published a book in 1928 entitled *Political Behavior, The Heretofore Unwritten Laws, Customs, and Principles of Politics as Practised in the United States*.[2] To Kent, the study of political behavior meant the cynical "realism" of the tough-minded newspaperman who reports the way things "really" happen and not the way they're supposed to happen. This meaning, I may say, is often implied even today. However, Herbert Tingsten rescued the term for political science in 1937 by publishing his path-breaking *Political Behavior: Studies in Election Statistics*. Despite the fact that Tingsten was a Swede, and his work dealt with European elections, the term became increasingly identified with American political science.

The rapid flowering of the behavioral approach in the United States no doubt depended on the existence of some key attitudes and predispositions generated in the American culture—pragmatism, factmindedness, confidence in science, and the like.[3] But there were also at least six specific, interrelated, quite powerful stimuli.

One was Charles E. Merriam. In his presidential address to the American Political Science Association in 1925, Merriam said: "Some day we may take another angle of approach *than the formal, as other sciences do,* and begin to look at *political behavior* as one of the essential objects of inquiry."[4]

During the next decade under Merriam's leadership at the University of Chicago, the Department of Political Science was the center of what would later have been called the behavioral approach. A number of the political scientists who subsequently were widely regarded as leaders in introducing that approach into American political science were faculty members or graduate students there: for example, Harold Lasswell as a faculty member and V. O. Key, Jr., David Truman, Herbert Simon, and Gabriel Almond, all graduate students in Merriam's department before the Second World War. Chicago was not the only place where the new mood of scientific empiricism was strong. At Cornell University, for example, G. E. G. Catlin was expounding similar views.[5] But the collective impact of "the Chicago school" as it was sometimes called, was greater than that of a single scholar.

 A second force was the arrival in the United States in the 1930's of a considerable number of European scholars, particularly German refugees, who brought with them a sociological approach to politics that strongly reflected the specific influence of Max Weber and the general influence of European sociology. American political science had always been strongly influenced by Europeans. Not only have Americans often interpreted their own political institutions most clearly with the aid of sympathetic foreigners like de Tocqueville, Bryce, and Brogan, but American scholars have owed specific debts to European scholarship. The first American university chair in political science (actually in History and Political Science), established in 1858 at Columbia, was occupied by the liberal German refugee Francis Lieber. In the second half of the nineteenth century, many of the leading academic advocates of a "science of politics" sought to profit from the methods and teachings in some of the leading European universities.[6]

In the 1930's, there was once again an abrupt revival of European influences as the life of American universities was enriched by the great influx of refugee scholars.

A number of these scholars who came to occupy leading positions in departments of sociology and political science insisted on the relevance of sociological and even psychological theories for an understanding of politics. They drew attention to the importance of Marx, Durkheim, Freud, Pareto, Mosca, Weber, Michels, and others. Although some of them might later reject the behavioral approach precisely because they felt it was too narrow, men like Franz Neumann, Sigmund Neumann, Paul Lazarsfeld, Hans Speier, Hans Gerth, Reinhard Bendix, and many others exerted, both directly and indirectly, a profound influence on political research in the United States. Political sociology began to flourish. Political scientists discovered that their sociological colleagues were moving with speed and skill into areas they had long regarded as their own.

The Second World War also stimulated the development of the behavioral approach in the United States, for a great many American political scientists temporarily vacated their ivory towers and came to grips with day-to-day political and administrative realities in Washington and elsewhere: a whole generation of American political science later drew on these experiences. The confrontation of theory and reality provoked, in most of the men who performed their stint in Washington or elsewhere, a strong sense of the inadequacies of the conventional approaches of political science for describing reality, much less for predicting in any given situation what was likely to happen.

Possibly an even bigger impetus—not unrelated to the effects of the War—was provided by the Social Science Research Council, which has had an unostentatious but cumulatively enormous impact on American social science. A leading spirit in the Council for the past two decades has been a distinguished political scientist, E. Pendleton Herring. His own work before he assumed the presidency of the Council in 1948 reflected a concern for realism, for breaking the bonds of research confined entirely to the library, and for individual and group influences on politics and administration. In the mid-1940's Herring was instrumental in creating an SSRC committee on political behavior. The Annual Report of the SSRC for 1944–45 indicated that the Council had reached a

> . . . decision to explore the feasibility of developing a new approach to *the study of political behavior*. Focused upon *the behavior of individuals* in political situations, this approach calls for examination of the political relationships of men—as citizens, administrators, and legislators—by disciplines which can throw light on the problems involved, with the object of *formulating and testing hypotheses,* concerning *uniformities of behavior* in different institutional settings. (Emphasis added.)

In 1945 the Council established a Committee on Political Behavior, with Herring as the chairman. The three other members[7] were also well-known political scientists with a definite concern about the state of conventional political science. In 1949, the Council, together with the University of Michigan's Department of Political Science and its Institute for Social Research, held a week's conference on Research on Political Behavior at Ann Arbor. The topics covered help to provide an implicit definition of the term: papers were presented on regional politics, the possible contributions of related social sciences (*e.g.,* George P. Murdoch, the anthropologist, discussed the "Possibility of a General Social Science of Government"), voting behavior, political attitudes, groups, and methodological problems.[8]

Near the end of 1949, a new SSRC Committee on Political Behavior was appointed, with V. O. Key, Jr., as the chairman. In 1950, this committee succinctly defined its task: "The committee is concerned with the *development of theory* and *improvement in methods* which are needed if *social science research* on the *political process* is to be more effective."[9] This committee has been an active stimulant in the growth of the behavioral approach down to the present time; indeed, in recent years (under the chairmanship of David Truman) the committee has also awarded research grants.

The fifth factor was the rapid growth of the "survey" method as a tool available for the study of political choices and attitudes, and specifically of the behavior of voters. Where Tingsten had necessarily relied on aggregate voting statistics, the survey method provided direct access to the characteristics and behavior of individuals: an advantage that anyone who has ever labored with aggregate data is quick to recognize. As survey methods became more and more "scientific," particularly under the auspices of the Survey Research Center of the University of Michigan and the Bureau of Applied Social Research at Columbia, political scientists found their presumed monopoly of skills in the scholarly interpretation of voting and elections rudely destroyed by sociologists and social psychologists who in a series of pathbreaking studies of presidential elections began to convert the analysis of voting from impressionistic —even when it was brilliant—history or insightful journalism to a more pedestrian but occasionally more impressive and convincing empirical science. To political scientists dissatisfied with the conventional methods and manners of the discipline, the new voting studies offered encouragement. For in spite of obvious defects, the voting studies seemed to provide ground for the hope that if political scientists could only master the tools employed in the other social sciences— survey methods and statistical analysis, for example—they might be able to go beyond plausible generalities and proceed to test hypotheses about how people in fact do behave in making political choices.

A sixth factor that needs to be mentioned is the influence of those uniquely American institutions, the great philanthropic foundations—especially Carnegie, Rockefeller, and more recently Ford—which, because of their enormous financial contributions to scholarly research, and the inevitable selection among competing proposals that these entail, exert a considerable effect on the scholarly community. The relationship between foundation policy and current trends in academic research is too complex for facile generalities. Perhaps the simplest accurate statement is that the relationship is to a very high degree reciprocal: the staffs of the foundations are highly sensitive to the views of distinguished scholars, on whom they rely heavily for advice, and at the same time because even foundation resources are scarce, the policies of foundation staffs and trustees must inevitably encourage or facilitate some lines of research more than others. If the foundations had been hostile to the behavioral approach, there can be no doubt that it would have had very rough sledding indeed. For characteristically, behavioral research costs a good deal more than is needed by the single scholar in the library—and sometimes, as with the studies of voting in presidential elections, behavioral research is enormously expensive.

In the period after the Second World War, however, the foundations—reflecting important trends within the social sciences themselves, stimulated by the factors I have already mentioned—tended to view interdisciplinary and behavioral studies with sympathy. The Rockefeller Foundation, for example, had helped finance the pioneering panel study by Lazarsfeld, Berelson, and Gaudet of voting in the 1940 presidential election in Erie County, Ohio, and it has also, almost singlehandedly, financed the costly election studies of the Survey Research Center at the University of Michigan. In the newest and richest foundation, Ford, the short-lived Behavioral Sciences Program probably increased the use and acceptability of the notion of behavioral sciences as something both more behavioral and more scientific than the social sciences (I confess the distinction still remains cloudy to me despite the earnest attempts of a number of behavioral scientists to set me straight). The most durable offshoot of the Behavioral Sciences Program at Ford is the Center for Advanced Study in the Behavioral Sciences at Palo Alto. Although the Center has often construed its domain in most catholic fashion—the "fellows" in any given year may include mathematicians, philosophers, historians, or even a novelist—in its early years the political scientists who were fellows there tended to be discontented with traditional approaches, inclined toward a more rigorously empirical and scientific study of politics, and deeply interested in learning wherever possible from the other social sciences.

All these factors, and doubtless others, came to fruition in the decade of the 1950's. The behavioral approach grew from the deviant and unpopular views of a minor sect into a major influence. Many of the radicals of the 1930's (professionally speaking) had, within two decades, become established leaders in American political science.

Today, many American departments of political science (including my own) offer undergraduate or graduate courses in Political Behavior. Indeed, in at least one institution (the University of Michigan) Political Behavior is not only a course but a field of graduate study parallel with such conventional fields as political theory, public administration, and the like—and recently buttressed, I note enviously, with some fat fellowships.

The presidency of the American Political Science Association furnishes a convenient symbol of the change. From 1927, when Merriam was elected president, until 1950, none of the presidents was prominently identified as an advocate of the behavioral approach. The election of Peter Odegard in 1950 might be regarded as the turning point. Since that time, the presidency has been occupied by one of Merriam's most brilliant and intellectually unconventional students, Harold Lasswell, and by three of the four members of the first SSRC Committee on Political Behavior.

Thus the revolutionary sectarians have found themselves,

perhaps more rapidly than they thought possible, becoming members of the Establishment.

II

I have not, however, answered the naggging question I set out to answer, though perhaps I have furnished some materials from which an answer might be derived. What *is* the behavioral approach in political science?

Historically speaking, the behavioral approach was a protest movement within political science. Through usage by partisans, partly as an epithet, terms like political behavior and the behavioral approach came to be associated with a number of political scientists, mainly Americans, who shared a strong sense of dissatisfaction with the achievements of conventional political science, particularly through historical, philosophical, and the descriptive-institutional approaches, and a belief that additional methods and approaches either existed or could be developed that would help to provide political science with empirical propositions and theories of a systematic sort, tested by closer, more direct, and more rigorously controlled observations of political events.

At a minimum, then, those who were sometimes called "Behaviorists" or "Behavioralists" shared a mood: a mood of skepticism about the current intellectual attainments of political science, a mood of sympathy toward "scientific" modes of investigation and analysis, a mood of optimism about the possibilities of improving the study of politics.

Was—or is—the behavioral approach ever anything more than this mood? Are there perhaps definite beliefs, assumptions, methods or topics that can be identified as constituting political behavior or the behavioral approach?

There are, so far as I can tell, three different answers to this question among those who employ the term carefully. The first answer is an unequivocal yes. Political behavior is said to refer to the study of *individuals* rather than larger political units. This emphasis is clear in the 1944–45 SSRC report (which I quoted earlier) that foreshadowed the creation of the Political Behavior Committee. This was also how David Easton defined the term in his searching analysis and criticism of American political science published in 1953.[10] In this sense, Tingsten, Lasswell, and studies of voting behavior are prime examples of the behavioral approach.

The second answer is an unequivocal no. In his recent *Political Science: A Philosophical Analysis* (1960), Vernon Van Dyke remarks: "Though stipulative definitions of *political behavior* are sometimes advanced, as when a course or a book is given this title, none of them has gained general currency."[11] Probably the most eloquent and resounding "No!" was supplied three years ago by an editorial in PROD, a journal that some American political scientists—and many of its readers—probably regarded as the authentic spokesman for the newest currents among the *avant garde* of political behavior. As an alumnus both of Merriam's Chicago department and the SSRC Committee on Political Behavior, the editor of PROD, Alfred de Grazia, could be presumed to speak with authority. He denied that the term referred to a subject matter, an interdisciplinary focus, quantification, any specific effort at new methods, behaviorist psychology, "realism" as opposed to "idealism," empiricism in contrast with deductive systems, or voting behavior—or, in fact, to anything more than political science as something that some people might like it to be. He proposed that the term be dropped.[12]

The third view is perhaps no more than an elaboration of the mood I mentioned a moment ago. In this view the behavioral approach is an attempt to improve our understanding of politics by seeking to explain the empirical aspects of political life by means of methods, theories, and criteria of proof that are acceptable according to the canons, conventions, and assumptions of modern empirical science.

In this sense, "a behavioral approach," as one writer recently observed, "is distinguished predominantly by the nature of the purpose it is designed to serve. The purpose is scientific. . . ."[13]

If we consider the behavioral approach in political science as simply an attempt to make the empirical component of the discipline more scientific, as that term is generally understood in the empirical sciences, much of the history that I have referred to falls into place. In a wise, judicious, and until very recently neglected essay entitled "The Implications of Political Behavior Research," David Truman, writing in 1951, set out the fruits of a seminar on political behavior research held at the University of Chicago in the summer of 1951. I think it is not misleading to say that the views Truman set forth in 1951 have been shared in the years since then by the members of the Committee on Political Behavior.

> Roughly defined, [he wrote] the term political behavior comprehends those actions and interactions of men and groups which are involved in the process of governing. . . . At the maximum this conception brings under the rubric of political behavior any human activities which can be said to be a part of governing.
>
> Properly speaking, political behavior is not a "field" of social science; it is not even a field of political science.
>
> . . . Political behavior is not and should not be a specialty, for it represents rather an orientation or a point of view which aims at *stating all the phenomena of government in terms of the observed and observable behavior of men.* To treat it as a "field" coordinate with (and presumably isolated from) public law, state and local government, international relations, and so on, would be to defeat its major aim. That aim includes an eventual reworking and extension of most of the conventional "fields" of political science. . . .
>
> The developments underlying the current interest in political behavior imply two basic requirements for adequate research. In the first place, research must be systematic. . . . This means that research must grow out of a precise statement of hypotheses and a rigorous ordering of evidence. . . . In the second place, research in political behavior must place primary em-

phasis upon empirical methods. . . . Crude empiricism, unguided by adequate theory, is almost certain to be sterile. Equally fruitless is speculation which is not or cannot be put to empirical test.

> . . . *The ultimate goal of the student of political behavior is the development of a science of the political process.* . . .[14]

Truman called attention to the advantages of drawing on the other social sciences and cautioned against indiscriminate borrowings. He argued that the "political behavior orientation . . . necessarily aims at being quantitative wherever possible. But . . . the student of political behavior . . . deals with the political institution and he is obliged to perform his task in *quantitative terms if he can and in qualitative terms if he must*." (Emphasis added.) He agreed that "inquiry into how men *ought* to act is not a concern of research in political behavior" but insisted on the importance of studying values as "obviously important determinants of men's behavior."

> Moreover, in political behavior research, as in the natural sciences, the values of the investigator are important in the selection of the objects and lines of inquiry. . . . A major reason for any inquiry into political behavior is to discover uniformities, and through discovering them to be better able to indicate the consequences of such patterns and of public policy, existing or proposed, for the maintenance or development of a preferred system of political values.

Truman denied that "the political behavior orientation implies a rejection of historical knowledge. . . . Historical knowledge is likely to be an essential supplement to contemporary observation of political behavior." Finally, while suggesting that the conventional graduate training of political scientists needed to be supplemented and modified, Truman emphatically opposed the notion that the behavioral approach required "the elimination of . . . traditional training."

Any new departure in an established discipline must build upon the accomplishments of the past. Although much of the existing literature of politics may be impressionistic, it is extensive and rich in insights. Without a command of the significant portions of that literature, behavioral research . . . is likely to be naive and unproductive. . . . Many attempts made by persons not familiar with the unsystematized facts [have been] substantively naive even when they may have been methodologically sound.

I have cited Truman's views at length for several reasons: because I wholeheartedly agree with them; because they were expressed a decade ago when the advocates of the behavioral approach were still searching for acceptance and self-definition; because they have been neglected; and because I believe that if the partisans and critics of "political behavior" and "the behavioral approach" had read them, understood them, and accepted them as a proper statement of objectives, much of the irrelevant, fruitless, and ill-informed debate over the behavioral approach over the past decade need never have occurred—or at any rate might have been conducted on a rather higher level of intellectual sophistication.

III

Thus the "behavioral approach" might better be called the "behavioral mood" or perhaps even the "scientific outlook."

Yet to explain the behavioral approach as nothing more or less than an emphasis on the term "science" in the phrase "political science" leaves unanswered whatever questions may be raised as to the present or potential achievements of this mood of protest, skepticism, reform, and optimism. Fortunately, there is an element of self-correction in intellectual life. The attempt to increase the scientific competence of political studies will inevitably be judged by results. And the judges of the next generation will share the skepticism of the past. If closer attention to methodological niceties, to problems of observation and verification, to the task of giving operational meaning to political concepts, to quantification and testing, to eliminating unproductive intervening variables, to sources of data, hypotheses, and theory in the other social sciences; if all of these activities do not yield explanations of some important aspects of politics that are more thoroughly verified, less open to methodological objections, richer in implications for further explanation, and more useful in meeting the perennial problems of political life than the explanations they are intended to replace; if, in short, the results of a scientific outlook do not measure up to the standards that serious students of politics have always attempted to apply, then we may confidently expect that the attempt to build an empirical science of politics will lose all the impetus in the next generation that it gained in the last.

The representatives of the "scientific outlook" are, it seems to me, right in saying that it is a little early to appraise the results. We shall need another generation of work before we can put the products of this new mood and outlook in political science in perspective. Nonetheless, I believe it may be useful to make a tentative if deliberately incomplete assessment.

The oldest and best example of the modern scientific outlook at work is to be found in studies of voting behavior using survey methods. These begin with *The People's Choice*,[15] a study of the 1940 presidential election first published in 1944, and end—for the moment at least—with the magnificent study of the 1956 election entitled *The American Voter*.[16] It is no exaggeration to say that in less than two decades this series of studies has significantly altered and greatly deepened our understanding of what in some ways is the most distinctive action for a citizen of democracy—deciding how to vote, or indeed whether to vote at all, in a competitive national election. Each study has profited from the last; and as broadly trained political scientists have begun to work on these studies together with sociologists and social psychologists, the contributions of the studies to our understanding of politics—rather than of individual psychology—have greatly increased. On many topics where only a generation ago we had not much beyond impressionistic evidence, today we can speak with some confidence.

Although in a field as ambiguous and rich in contradictory hypotheses as political science, it is nearly always possible to regard a finding as merely confirming the obvious, in fact a number of the findings point in rather unexpected directions: e.g., that "independent" voters tend to be less interested, involved, or informed than partisan voters;[17] that socio-economic "class" whether objectively or subjectively defined is not a factor of constant weight in American presidential elections but a variable subject to great swings; and that only a microscopic proportion of American voters can be said to bring any ideological perspectives, even loosely defined, to bear on their decisions. Where once one might have asserted these propositions or their contraries with equal plausibility, the evidence of the voting studies tends to pile up in a single direction. Moreover—and this is perhaps the most important point of all—these studies are cumulative. The early studies were highly incomplete and in many ways unsatisfactory. They were subject to a good deal of criticism, and properly so. Even the latest ones will not escape unharmed. Yet it seems to me there has been a steady and obvious improvement in quality, range, and depth.

The voting studies may have provided an indirect stimulus to the "scientific outlook" because of a psychological effect. It seems to be beyond much doubt that some political scientists, particularly younger ones, compared the yield produced by the methods used in the studies on voting with the normal yield of conventional methods and arrived at the inference—which is probably false—that the application of comparable new methods elsewhere could produce a comparable gain in results.

A closely related topic on which the scientific outlook has, in my view, produced some useful and reliable results of great importance to an understanding of politics is in the general domain of political participation. A listing of some of the chapter headings in Robert E. Lane's *Political Life* (1959) indicates the sort of question on which our knowledge is very much better off than it was only a few years ago: "Who Takes Part in Elections and What Do They Do?," "Who Tries to Influence Public Officials and How Do They Do It?," "Political Discussion: Who Listens to What? Who Talks to Whom?," "Why Lower-Status People Participate Less than Upper-Status People," "The Way of the Ethnic in Politics," etc.

Since I am not responsible for a complete inventory, I shall limit myself to mentioning one more subject where the behavioral mood has clearly made itself felt. This is in understanding the psychological characteristics of *homo politicus:* attitudes, beliefs, predispositions, personality factors. The range of "behavioral" scholars and research in this area is very great, though the researchers and the research may not always bear the professional label "political science." A few scattered names, titles, and topics will indicate what I have in mind: Lasswell, the great American pioneer in this area; Cantril; Lane; McClosky; Adorno, *et al., The Authoritarian Personality;* Almond, *The Appeals of Communism;* Stouffer, *Communism, Conformity and Civil Liberties;* and Lipset, "Working Class Authoritarianism" in *Political Man.* The fact that these scholars bear various professional labels—sociologist, psychologist, political scientist—and that it is not easy to read from the professional or departmental label of the author to the character of the work itself may be regarded by some political scientists as an appalling sign of disintegration in the distinctive properties of political science, but it is also a sign of the extent to which a concern by "behavioral scientists" with similar problems now tends to transcend (though not to eliminate entirely) differences in professional origins.

IV

What of the yield in other matters that have always been of concern to students of political life? There are a number of important aspects of political studies where the behavioral mood has had, is having, or probably soon will have an impact, but where we must reserve judgment for the time being simply because the results are too scanty.

A good example is the analysis of political *systems*. The most distinctive products of the behavioral mood so far have dealt with *individuals*—individuals who vote, participate in politics in other ways, or express certain attitudes or beliefs. But an individual is not a political system, and analysis of individual preferences cannot fully explain collective decisions, for in addition we need to understand the mechanisms by which individual decisions are aggregated and combined into collective decisions. We cannot move from a study of the attitudes of a random sample of American citizens to a reasonably full explanation of, say, presidential nominations or the persistent problems of policy coordination in the United States.

Yet one classic concern of students of politics has been the analysis of *systems* of individuals and groups. Although the impact of the scientific outlook on the study of political systems is still unclear, there are some interesting straws in the wind. In *Union Democracy,* Lipset, Trow, and Coleman brought the behavioral mood and the intellectual resources of three highly trained social scientists to bear on the task of explaining how it is that a legitimate two-party system is maintained, as it is not in other American trade unions, in the International Typographers' Union. Recently a number of political scientists have followed sociologists into the study of local communities as systems of influence or decision making.[18] Deutsch reflects the behavioral mood in his study of international political systems.[19] A number of other studies are in process that may help us formulate some new, or if not new then more persuasive, answers to some ancient questions.[20] But until more evidence is in, anyone who does not believe he knows *a priori* the outcome of this present expression of the scholar's age-old quest for knowledge will perhaps be pardoned if he reserves judgment and awaits the future with skepticism—mixed, depending on his prejudices, with hope or dread.

V

Where will the behavioral mood, considered as a movement of protest, go from here? I think it will gradually disappear. By this I mean only that it will slowly decay as a distinctive mood and outlook. For it will become, and in fact already is becoming, incorporated into the main body of the discipline. The behavioral mood will not disappear, then, because it has failed. It will disappear rather because it has succeeded. As a separate, somewhat sectarian, slightly factional outlook it will be the first victim of its own triumph.

Lest I be misunderstood in what I am about to say, let me make clear that the present and probable future benefits of the behavioral revolt to political studies seem to me to outweigh by far any disadvantages. In retrospect, the "behavioral" revolt in political science was, if anything, excessively delayed. Moreover, had that revolt not taken place, political science would have become increasingly alienated, I believe, from the other social sciences. One consequence of the behavioral protest has been to restore some unity within the social sciences by bringing political studies into closer affiliation with theories, methods, findings, and outlooks in modern psychology, sociology, anthropology, and economics.

But if the behavioral revolt in political science has helped to restore some unities, it has shattered others; and the fragments probably cannot ever again be united exactly along the old lines. There are, so to speak, five fragments in search of a unity. These are: empirical political science, standards of evaluation, history, general theory, and speculation.

The empirical political scientist is concerned with what *is,* as he says, not with what *ought* to be. Hence, he finds it difficult and uncongenial to assume the historic burden of the political philosopher who attempted to determine, prescribe, elaborate, and employ ethical standards—values, to use the fashionable term—in appraising political acts and political systems. The behaviorally minded student of politics is prepared to *describe* values as empirical data; but, qua "scientist" he seeks to avoid prescription or inquiry into the grounds on which judgments of value can properly be made. To whom, then, are we to turn for guidance on intricate questions of political appraisal and evaluation? Today, probably no single professional group is qualified to speak with wisdom on all important political alternatives.

It may be said that this is the task of the political philosopher. But the problem of the political philosopher who wishes to engage in political evaluation in a sophisticated way is rendered ever more formidable by the products of the behavioral mood. An act of political evaluation cannot be performed in a sterile medium free from contamination by brute facts. Surely no one today, for example, can intelligently consider the relative merits of different political systems, or different arrangements within a particular political system, unless he knows what there is to be known about how these systems or arrangements work, what is required to make them work, and what effects they have on participants. No doubt the specialist who "knows the facts" —whether as physicist, physician, or political scientist— sometimes displays great naiveté on matters of policy. Still, the impatience of the empirical political scientist with the political philosopher who insists upon the importance of "values" arises in part from a feeling that the political philosopher who engages in political evaluation rarely completes all his homework. The topic of "consensus" as a condition for democracy is a case in point; when the political philosopher deals with this question, it seems to me that he typically makes a number of assumptions and assertions of an empirical sort without systematic attention to existing empirical data, or the possibility of gaining better empirical data.[21] Obviously some division of labor will always be necessary in a field as broad as the study of politics, but clearly the field needs more people who do not regard rapid shifts of mood—I mean from the behavioral to the philosophical— as a symptom of severe schizophrenia.

Second, in his concern for analyzing what *is,* the behavioral political scientist has found it difficult to make systematic use of what *has been:* i.e., with history. In a trivial sense, of course, all knowledge of fact is historical; but I am speaking here of the history of the historian. Despite disclaimers and intentions to the contrary, there seems to me little room for doubt that the actual content of almost all the studies that reflect the behavioral mood is a-historical in character. Yet the scientific shortcomings of an a-historical theory in political science are manifest, and political scientists with "behavioral" predispositions are among the first to admit them. As the authors of *The American Voter* remark:

> In somewhat severe language, theory may be characterized as a generalized statement of the inter-relationships of a set of variables. In these terms, historical description may be said to be a statement of the values assumed by these variables through time. . . .
>
> If theory can guide historical descriptions, the historical context of most research on human behavior places clear limitations on the development of theory. In evolving and testing his theoretical hypotheses the social scientist usually must de-

pend on what he is permitted to observe by the progress of history. . . . It is evident that *variables of great importance in human affairs may exhibit little or no change in a given historical period.* As a result, the investigator whose work falls in this period *may not see the significance of these variables* and may fail to incorporate them in his theoretical statements. And even if he does perceive their importance, the *absence of variation will prevent a proper test of hypotheses* that state the relation of these factors to other variables of his theory (pp. 8–10; emphasis added).

There are, I think, a number of nodes around which a unity between behavioral political studies and history may be expected to grow. Because it is unreasonable to suppose that anything like the whole field of history will lend itself successfully to the behavioral approach, both historians and political scientists might profitably look for targets-of-opportunity on which the weapons forged by modern social science can be brought to bear. In this respect the work of the American historian Lee Benson seems to me particularly promising. By the application of rather elementary methods, which the historian has not been prone to employ, including very simple statistical analysis, Benson has shown how the explanations of five eminent American historians of four different presidential elections are dubious, if not, in fact, downright absurd.[22] The sociologist, S. M. Lipset, has also contributed a new interpretation of the 1860 election, based upon his analysis of Southern voting patterns in the presidential election of that year and in referenda on secession a few months later.[23] Benson has also turned his attention both to Charles A. Beard's famous interpretation—which Beard called an economic interpretation—of the creation and adoption of the American Constitution, and to the latter-day critics of Beard's somewhat loosely stated theory; he demonstrates convincingly, at least to me, some of the gains that can arise from a greater methodological sophistication on matters of causation, correlation, and use of quantitative data than is customary among professional historians.[24]

In addition to these targets-of-opportunity that occur here and there in historical studies, a problem that obviously needs the joint attention of historian and "behavioral" political scientist is the matter of political change. To the extent that the political scientist is interested in gaining a better understanding of political change—as, say, in the developing countries, to cite an example of pressing importance—he will have to work with theories that can only be fully tested against historical data. Unfortunately, the a-theoretical or even anti-theoretical biases of many historians often make their works a storehouse of data so vast as to be almost unmanageable for the theorist. Rather than demand that every theorist should have to become his own historian, it may be more feasible to demand that more historians should become theorists, or at any rate familiar with the most relevant issues, problems, and methods of the modern social sciences.

I have already implied the third unity that needs to be established, namely a unity between empirical political studies and a concern for general theory. The scientific outlook in political science can easily produce a dangerous and dysfunctional humility: the humility of the social scientist who may be quite confident of his findings on small matters and dubious that he can have anything at all to say on larger questions. The danger, of course, is that the quest for empirical data can turn into an absorbing search for mere trivialities unless it is guided by some sense of the difference between an explanation that would not matter much even if it could be shown to be valid by the most advanced methods now available, and one that would matter a great deal if it should turn out to be a little more or a little less plausible than before, even if it still remained in some considerable doubt. So far, I think, the impact of the scientific outlook has been to stimulate caution rather than boldness in searching for broad explanatory theories. The political scientist who mixes skepticism with methodological rigor is all too painfully aware of the inadequacies of any theory that goes much beyond the immediate data at hand. Yet it seems clear that unless the study of politics generates and is guided by broad, bold, even if highly vulnerable general theories, it is headed for the ultimate disaster of triviality.

Finally, I should like to suggest that empirical political science had better find a place for speculation. It is a grave though easy error for students of politics impressed by the achievements of the natural sciences to imitate all their methods save the most critical one: the use of the imagination. Problems of method and a proper concern for what would be regarded as an acceptable test of an empirical hypothesis have quite properly moved out of the wings to a more central position on the great stage of political science. Yet surely it is imagination that has generally marked the intelligence of the great scientist, and speculation—often-times foolish speculation, it turned out later—has generally preceded great advances in scientific theory. It is only fair to add, however, that the speculation of a Galileo, a Kepler, a Newton, or an Einstein was informed and controlled by a deep understanding of the hard empirical facts as they were known at the time: Kepler's speculations always had to confront the tables of Tycho Brahe.

There is every reason to think that unities can be forged anew. After all, as the names of Socrates, Aristotle, Machiavelli, Hobbes, and Tocqueville remind us, from time to time in the past the study of politics has been altered, permanently, by a fresh infusion of the spirit of empirical inquiry —by, that is to say, the scientific outlook.

REFERENCES

1. David Easton, *The Political System* (New York: Alfred A. Knopf, 1953), p. 203.
2. Kent's earlier book, *The Great Game of Politics* (1924), made no pretence of being systematic and continued to be widely read

by students of American politics, but within a few years *Political Behavior* fell into an obscurity from which it has never recovered.

3. *Cf.* Bernard Crick, *The American Science of Politics, Its Origins and Conditions* (London, 1959).

4. "Progress in Political Research," *American Political Science Review*, 20 (February 1926), 7, quoted in David B. Truman, "The Implications of Political Behavior Research," *Social Science Review Council Items*, 5 (December 1951), 37. Emphasis added.

5. See Catlin's *Science and Method of Politics* (1927). Another early example of the behavioral approach was Stuart Rice, *Quantitative Methods in Politics* (1928). Rice had received his Ph.D. at Columbia University.

6. *Cf.* Bernard Crick, *op. cit.*, pp. 21–31. Crick notes that "The Fifth Volume of the Johns Hopkins University *Studies in Historical and Political Science* published a long study, edited by Andrew D. White, 'European Schools of History and Politics' (December 1887). It reprinted his Johns Hopkins address on 'Education in Political Science' together with reports on 'what we can learn from' each major European country." Fn. 1, p. 27.

7. Herbert Emmerich, Charles S. Hyneman, and V. O. Key, Jr.

8. Alexander Heard, "Research on Political Behavior: Report of a Conference," *Social Science Research Council Items*, 3 (December 1949), 41–44.

9. *Social Science Research Council Items*, 4 (June 1950), 20. (Italics added.)

10. "To precisely what kind of research does the concept of political behavior refer? It is clear that this term indicates that the research worker wishes to look at participants in the political system as individuals who have the emotions, prejudices, and predispositions of human beings as we know them in our daily lives. . . . Behavioral research . . . has therefore sought to elevate the actual human being to the center of attention. Its premise is that the traditionalists have been reifying institutions, virtually looking at them as entities apart from their component individuals. . . . Research workers often use the terms . . . to indicate that they are studying the political process by looking at the relation of it to the motivations, personalities, or feelings of the participants as individual human beings." David Easton, *The Political System* (1953), pp. 201–205.

11. As we shall see, Van Dyke distinguishes the term "behavioral approach" from "political behavior."

12. "What Is Political Behavior?," PROD (July 1958).

13. *Ibid.*, p. 159.

14. *Social Science Research Council Items*, 5 (December 1951), 37–39. (Italics added.)

15. Paul F. Lazarsfeld, Bernard Berelson, and Hazel Gaudet, *The People's Choice* (New York: Columbia University Press, 1944).

16. Angus Campbell, Philip Converse, Donald Stokes, and Warren Miller, *The American Voter* (New York: John Wiley, 1960), a study extended and refined by the same authors in "Stability and Change in 1960: A Reinstating Election," *American Political Science Review* 55 (1961), 269–80.

17. A finding, incidentally, that may have to be revised in turn. A

recent reanalysis of the data of the voting studies, completed after this paper was prepared, has turned up new evidence for the active, interested independent voter. William Flanigan, *Partisanship and Campaign Participation* (Ph.D. dissertation; Yale University Library, 1961).

18. *Cf.* Janowitz, ed., *Community Political Systems* (New York: The Free Press, 1961); Edward Banfield, *Political Influence* (New York: The Free Press, 1961); and the English study by Birch and his colleagues at the University of Manchester, *Small Town Politics* (1959).

19. E.g., in his *Nationalism and Social Communication* (1953). See also his recent article with the economist Alexander Eckstein, "National Industrialization and the Declining Share of the International Economic Sector, 1890–1959," *World Politics* (January 1961), pp. 267–99; and his "Social Mobilization and Political Development," *American Political Science Review*, 55 (September 1961), 493–514.

20. For an interesting example of an application of the behavioral mood to comparative politics, see Stein Rokkan and Henry Valen, "Parties, Elections and Political Behavior in the Northern Countries: a Review of Recent Research," *Politische Forschung* (1960). Probably the most ambitious attempt to apply survey methods to comparative politics is represented by a study of political socialization and political values in five nations, conducted by Gabriel A. Almond; see Almond and Verba, *The Civic Culture* (Princeton: Princeton University Press, 1963).

21. In 1942, in *The New Belief in the Common Man* (Boston: Beacon Press), C. J. Friedrich challenged the prevailing generalizations about the need for consensus (chapt. 5). However, his challenge seems to have met with little response until 1960, when Prothro and Grigg reported the results of an empirical study of consensus on "democratic" propositions in Ann Arbor, Michigan, and Tallahassee, Florida. See their "Fundamental Principles of Democracy," *Journal of Politics*, 22 (May 1960), 276–94.

22. The historians and the elections were: Arthur Schlesinger, Jr., on the election of 1824, Samuel E. Morison and Henry S. Commager on the election of 1860, Alan Nevins on the election of 1884, and William Diamond on the election of 1896. See his "Research Problems in American Political Historiography," in Komarovsky, ed., *Common Frontiers of the Social Sciences* (New York: The Free Press, 1957).

23. "The Emergence of the One-Party South—the Election of 1860" in *Political Man* (New York: Doubleday, 1960).

24. Lee Benson, *Turner and Beard, American Historical Writing Reconsidered* (New York: The Free Press, 1960).

4: *What Is Political Philosophy? The Problem of Political Philosophy*

LEO STRAUSS

The meaning of political philosophy and its meaningful character are as evident today as they have been since the time when political philosophy first made its appearance in Athens. All political action aims at either preservation or change. When desiring to preserve, we wish to prevent a change to the worse; when desiring to change, we wish to bring about something better. All political action is, then, guided by some thought of better or worse. But thought of better or worse implies thought of the good. The awareness of the good which guides all our actions has the character of opinion: it is no longer questioned but, on reflection, it proves to be questionable. The very fact that we can question it directs us toward such a thought of the good

Reprinted from *The Journal of Politics*, 19 (August 1957), 343–55, by permission of the author and the publisher. The article as it appeared in that journal was a revised version of a portion of the Judah L. Magnes Lectures delivered at the Hebrew University in Jerusalem in December 1945 and January 1955. A Hebrew translation with an English summary of this version appeared in *Iyyun*, April 1955.

as is no longer questionable—toward a thought which is no longer opinion but knowledge. All political action has then in itself a directedness toward knowledge of the good: of the good life, or the good society. For the good society is the complete political good.

If this directedness becomes explicit, if men make it their explicit goal to acquire knowledge of the good life and of the good society, political philosophy emerges. By calling this pursuit political philosophy, we imply that it forms a part of a larger whole: of philosophy. Since political philosophy is a branch of philosophy, even the most provisional explanation of what political philosophy is cannot dispense with an explanation, however provisional, of what philosophy is. Philosophy, as quest for wisdom, is quest for universal knowledge, for knowledge of the whole. The quest would not be necessary if such knowledge were immediately available. The absence of knowledge of the whole does not mean, however, that men do not have thoughts about the whole: philosophy is necessarily preceded by opinions about the whole. It is, therefore, the attempt to replace opinions about the whole by knowledge of the whole. Instead of "the whole" philosophers also say "all things"; the whole is not a pure ether or an unrelieved darkness in which one cannot distinguish one part from the other, or in which one cannot discern anything. A quest for knowledge of "all things" means quest for knowledge of God, the world, and man—or rather, quest for knowledge of the natures of all things: the natures in their totality are "the whole."

Philosophy is essentially not possession of the truth, but quest for the truth. The distinctive trait of the philosopher is that "he knows nothing," and that his insight into our ignorance concerning the most important things induces him to strive with all his power for knowledge. He would cease to be a philosopher by evading the questions concerning those things or by disregarding them because they cannot be answered. It may be that as regards the possible answers to these questions, the pros and cons will always be in a more or less even balance, and, therefore, the stage of discussion or disputation will never reach the stage of decision. This would not make philosophy futile. For the clear grasp of a fundamental question requires understanding of the nature of the subject matter with which the question is concerned. Genuine knowledge of a fundamental question, thorough understanding of it, is better than blindness to it, or indifference to it, be that indifference or blindness accompanied by knowledge of the answers to a vast number of peripheral or ephemeral questions or not.

Of philosophy thus understood, political philosophy is a branch. Political philosophy will then be the attempt to replace opinion about the nature of political things by knowledge of the nature of political things. Political things are by their nature subject to approval and disapproval, to choice and rejection, to praise and blame. It is of their essence not to be neutral but to raise a claim to men's obedience, allegiance, decision or judgment. One does not understand them as what they are, as political things, if one does not take seriously their explicit or implicit claim to be judged in terms of goodness or badness, of justice or injustice; i.e., if one does not measure them by some standard of goodness or justice. To judge soundly one must know the true standards. If political philosophy wishes to do justice to its subject matter, it must strive for genuine knowledge of these standards. Political philosophy is the attempt truly to know both the nature of political things and the right, or the good, political order.

All knowledge of political things implies assumptions concerning the nature of political things; i.e., assumptions which concern not merely the given political situation but political life or human life as such. One cannot know anything about a war going on at a given time without having some notion, however dim and hazy, of war as such and its place within human life as such. One cannot see a policeman as a policeman without having made an assumption about law and government as such. The assumptions concerning the nature of political things, which are implied in all knowledge of political things, have the character of opinions. It is only when these assumptions are made the theme of critical and coherent analysis that a philosophic or scientific approach to politics emerges.

The cognitive status of political knowledge is not different from that of knowledge possessed by the shepherd, the husband, the general, or the cook. Yet the pursuits of these types of man do not give rise to pastoral, marital, military, or culinary philosophy because their ultimate goals are sufficiently clear and unambiguous. The ultimate political goal, on the other hand, urgently calls for coherent reflection. The goal of the general is victory, whereas the goal of the statesman is the common good. What victory means is not essentially controversial, but the meaning of the common good is essentially controversial. The ambiguity of the political goal is due to its comprehensive character. Thus the temptation arises to deny, or to evade, the comprehensive character of politics and to treat politics as one compartment among many. This temptation must be resisted if we are to face our situation as human beings; i.e., the whole situation.

Political philosophy as we have tried to circumscribe it, has been cultivated since its beginnings almost without any interruption until a relatively short time ago. Today, political philosophy is in a state of decay and perhaps of putrefaction, if it has not vanished altogether. Not only is there complete disagreement regarding its subject matter, its methods, and its function; its very possibility in any form has become questionable. The only point regarding which academic teachers of political science still agree concerns the usefulness of studying the history of political philosophy. As regards the philosophers, it is sufficient to contrast the work of the four greatest philosophers of the last forty years—Bergson, Whitehead, Husserl, and Heidegger—with the work of Hermann

Cohen in order to see how rapidly and thoroughly political philosophy has become discredited. We may describe the present situation as follows. Originally political philosophy was identical with political science, and it was the all-embracing study of human affairs. Today, we find it cut into pieces which behave as if they were parts of a worm. In the first place, one has applied the distinction between philosophy and science to the study of human affairs, and accordingly one makes a distinction between a nonphilosophical political science and a nonscientific political philosophy, a distinction which under present conditions takes away all dignity, all honesty from political philosophy. Furthermore, large segments of what formerly belonged to political philosophy or political science have become emancipated under the names of economics, sociology, and social psychology. The pitiable rump for which honest social scientists do not care is left as prey to philosophers of history and to people who amuse themselves more than others with professions of faith. We hardly exaggerate when we say that today political philosophy does not exist anymore, except as matter for burial—i.e., for historical research—or else as a theme of weak and unconvincing protestations.

If we inquire into the reasons for this great change, we receive these answers: political philosophy is unscientific, or it is unhistorical, or it is both. Science and History, those two great powers of the modern world, have eventually succeeded in destroying the very possibility of political philosophy.

The rejection of political philosophy as unscientific is characteristic of present-day positivism. Positivism is no longer what it desired to be when Auguste Comte originated it. It still agrees with Comte by maintaining that modern science is the highest form of knowledge, precisely because it aims no longer, as theology and metaphysics did, at absolute knowledge of the Why, but only at relative knowledge of the How. But after having been modified by utilitarianism, evolutionism, and neo-Kantianism, it has abandoned completely Comte's hope that a social science modeled on modern natural science would be able to overcome the intellectual anarchy of modern society. In about the last decade of the nineteenth century, social science positivism reached its final form by realizing, or decreeing, that there is a fundamental difference between facts and values, and that only factual judgments are within the competence of science: scientific social science is incompetent to pronounce value judgments, and must avoid value judgments altogether. As for the meaning of the term "value" in statements of this kind, we can hardly say more than that "values" mean both things preferred and principles of preference.

A discussion of the tenets of social science positivism is today indispensable for explaining the meaning of political philosophy. We must reconsider especially the practical consequences of this positivism. Positivistic social science is "value-free" or "ethically neutral": it is neutral in the conflict between good and evil, however good and evil may be understood. This means that the ground which is common to all social scientists, the ground on which they carry on their investigations and discussions, can only be reached through a process of emancipation from moral judgments, or of abstracting from moral judgments: moral obtuseness is the necessary condition for scientific analysis. For to the extent to which we are not yet completely insensitive to moral distinctions, we are forced to make value judgments. The habit of looking at social or human phenomena without making value judgments has a corroding influence on any preferences. The more serious we are as social scientists, the more completely we develop within ourselves a state of indifference to any goal, or of aimlessness and drifting, a state which may be called nihilism. The social scientist is not immune to preferences; his activity is a constant fight against the preferences he has as a human being and a citizen and which threaten to overcome his scientific detachment. He derives the power to counteract these dangerous influences by his dedication to one and only one value—to truth. But according to his principles, truth is not a value which it is necessary to choose: one may reject it as well as choose it. The scientist as scientist must indeed have chosen it. But neither scientists nor science are simply necessary. Social science cannot pronounce on the question of whether social science itself is good. It is then compelled to teach that society can with equal right and with equal reason favor social science as well as suppress it as disturbing, subversive, corrosive, nihilistic. But strangely enough we find social scientists very anxious to "sell" social science; i.e., to prove that social science is necessary. They will argue as follows. Regardless of what our preferences or ends may be, we wish to achieve our ends; to achieve our ends, we must know what means are conducive to our ends; but adequate knowledge of the means conducive to any social ends is the sole function of social science and only of social science; hence social science is necessary for any society or any social movement; social science is then simply necesary; it is a value from every point of view. But once we grant this we are seriously tempted to wonder if there are not a few other things which must be values from every point of view or for every thinking human being. To avoid this inconvenience the social scientist will scorn all considerations of public relations or of private advancement, and take refuge in the virtuous contention that he does not know, but merely believes that quest for truth is good: other men may believe with equal right that quest for truth is bad. But what does he mean by this contention? Either he makes a distinction between noble and ignoble objectives or he refuses to make such a distinction. If he makes a distinction between noble and ignoble objectives he will say there is a variety of noble objectives or of ideals, and that there is no ideal which is compatible with all other ideals: if one chooses truth as one's ideal, one necessarily rejects other ideals; this being the case, there cannot be a necessity, an evident necessity for noble men to choose truth in preference to other ideals. But as long as the social scientist speaks of ideals, and thus makes a distinction between noble and not noble objectives, or between idealistic integrity and petty egoism, he makes a value judgment which according to his fundamental contention is, as such, no longer necessary. He must then say that it is as legitimate to make the pursuit of safety, income, deference, one's sole aim in life, as it is to make the quest for truth one's chief aim. He thus lays himself open to the suspicion that his activity as a social scientist serves no other purpose than to increase his safety, his income, and his prestige, or that his competence as a social scientist is a skill which he is prepared to sell to the highest bidder. Honest citizens will begin to wonder whether such a man can be trusted, or whether he can be loyal, especially since he must maintain that it is as defensible to choose loyalty as one's value as it is to reject it. In a word, he will get entangled in the predicament which leads to the downfall of Thrasymachus and his taming by Socrates in the first book of Plato's *Republic*.

It goes without saying that while our social scientist may be confused, he is very far from being disloyal and from lacking integrity. His assertion that integrity and quest for truth are values which one can with equal right choose or reject is a mere movement of his lips and his tongue, to which nothing corresponds in his heart or mind. I have never met any scientific social scientist who, apart from being dedicated to truth and integrity, was not also wholeheartedly devoted to democracy. When he says that democracy is a value which is not evidently superior to the opposite value, he does not mean that he is impressed by the alternative which he rejects, or that his heart or his mind are torn between alternatives which in themselves are equally attractive. His "ethical neutrality" is so far from being nihilism or a road to nihilism that it is not more than an alibi for thoughtlessness and vulgarity: by saying that democracy and truth are values, he says in effect that one does not have to think about the reasons why these things are good, and that he may bow as well as anyone else to the values that are adopted and respected by his society. Social science positivism fosters not so much nihilism as conformism and philistinism.

It is not necessary to enter here and now into a discussion of the theoretical weaknesses of social science positivism. It suffices to allude to the considerations which speak decisively against this school.

1. It is impossible to study social phenomena—i.e., all important social phenomena—without making value judgments. A man who sees no reason for not despising people whose horizon is limited to their consumption of food and their digestion may be a tolerable econometrist; he cannot say anything relevant about the character of human society. A man who refuses to distinguish between great statesmen, mediocrities, and insane imposters may be a good bibliographer; he cannot say anything relevant about politics and political history. A man who cannot distinguish between a profound religious thought and a languishing superstition may be a good statistician; he cannot say anything relevant about the sociology of religion. Generally speaking, it is impossible to understand thought or action or work without evaluating it. If we are unable to evaluate adequately, as we very frequently are, we have not yet succeeded in understanding adequately. The value judgments which are forbidden to enter through the front door of political science, sociology, or economics enter these disciplines through the back door; they come from that annex of present day social science which is called psychopathology. Social scientists see themselves compelled to speak of unbalanced, neurotic, maladjusted people. But these value judgments are distinguished from those used by the great historians, not by greater clarity or certainty, but merely by their poverty: a slick operator is as well adjusted as, he may be better adjusted than, a good man or a good citizen. Finally, we must not overlook

the invisible value judgments which are concealed from undiscerning eyes but nevertheless most effective in allegedly purely descriptive concepts. For example, when social scientists distinguish between democratic and authoritarian habits or types of human beings, what they call "authoritarian" is in all cases known to me as a caricature of everything of which they, as good democrats of a certain kind, disapprove. Or when they speak of three principles of legitimacy, rational, traditional, and charismatic, their very expression "routinization of charisma" betrays a Protestant or liberal preference which no conservative Jew and no Catholic would accept: in the light of the notion of "routinization of charisma," the genesis of the Halakah out of Biblical prophecy, on the one hand, and the genesis of the Catholic Church out of the New Testament teaching necessarily appear as cases of "routinization of charisma." If the objection should be made that value judgments are indeed inevitable in social science but have a merely conditional character, I would reply as follows: are the conditions in question not necessarily fulfilled when we are interested in social phenomena? Must the social scientist not necessarily make the assumption that a healthy social life in this world is good, just as medicine necessarily makes the assumption that health and a healthy long life are good? And also are not all factual assertions based on conditions, or assumptions, which, however, do not become questionable as long as we deal with facts qua facts (e.g., that there are "facts," that events have causes)?

The impossibility of a "value-free" political science can be shown most simply as follows. Political science presupposes a distinction between political things and things which are not political; it presupposes therefore some answer to the question "what is political?" In order to be truly scientific, political science would have to raise this question and to answer it explicitly and adequately. But it is impossible to define the political—i.e., that which is related in a relevant way to the *polis,* the "country" or the "state"—without answering the question of what constitutes this kind of society. Now, a society cannot be defined without reference to its purpose. The most well known attempt to define "the state" without regard to its purpose admittedly led to a definition which was derived from "the modern type of state" and which is fully applicable only to that type; it was an attempt to define the modern state without having first defined the state. But by defining the state, or rather civil society, with reference to its purpose, one admits a standard in the light of which one must judge political actions and institutions: the purpose of civil society necessarily functions as a standard for judging of civil societies.

2. The rejection of value judgments is based on the assumption that the conflicts between different values or value systems are essentially insoluble for human reason. But this assumption, while generally taken to be sufficiently established, has never been proven. Its proof would require an effort of the magnitude of that which went into the conception and elaboration of the *Critique of Pure Reason;* it would require a comprehensive critique of evaluating reason. What we find in fact are sketchy observations which pretend to prove that this or that specific value conflict is insoluble. It is prudent to grant that there are value conflicts which cannot in fact be settled by human reason. But if we cannot decide which of two mountains whose peaks are hidden by clouds is higher than the other, cannot we decide that a mountain is higher than a molehill? If we cannot decide regarding a war between two neighboring nations, which have been fighting each other for centuries, whose nation's cause is more just, cannot we decide that Jezebel's action against Naboth was inexcusable? The greatest representative of social science positivism, Max Weber, has postulated the insolubility of all value conflicts because his soul craved a universe in which failure, that bastard of forceful sinning accompanied by still more forceful faith, instead of felicity and serenity, was to be the mark of human nobility. The

belief that value judgments are not subject, in the last analysis, to rational control encourages the inclination to make irresponsible assertions regarding right and wrong or good and bad. One evades serious discussion of serious issues by the simple device of passing them off as value problems. One even creates the impression that all important human conflicts are value conflicts, whereas, to say the least, many of these conflicts arise out of men's very agreement regarding values.

3. The belief that scientific knowledge—i.e., the kind of knowledge possessed or aspired to by modern science—is the highest form of human knowledge implies a depreciation of prescientific knowledge. If one takes into consideration the contrast between scientific knowledge of the world and prescientific knowledge of the world, one realizes that positivism preserves in a scarcely disguised manner Descartes' universal doubt of prescientific knowledge and his radical break with it. It certainly distrusts prescientific knowledge which it likes to compare to folklore. This superstition fosters all sorts of sterile investigations or complicated idiocies. Things which every ten year old child of normal intelligence knows are regarded as being in need of scientific proof in order to become acceptable as facts. And this scientific proof, which is not only not necessary, is not even possible. To illustrate this by the simplest example: all studies in social science presuppose that its devotees can tell human beings from other beings; this most fundamental knowledge was not acquired by them in classrooms; and this knowledge is not transformed by social science into scientific knowledge, but retains its initial status without any modification throughout. If this prescientific knowledge is not knowledge, all scientific studies which stand or fall with it lack the character of knowledge. The preoccupation with scientific proof of things which everyone knows well enough, and better, without scientific proof leads to the neglect of that thinking, or that reflection, which must precede all scientific studies if

these studies are to be relevant. The scientific study of politics is often presented as ascending from the ascertainment of political "facts"—i.e., of what has happened hitherto in politics—to the formulation of "laws" whose knowledge would permit the prediction of future political events. This goal is taken as a matter of course without a previous investigation as to whether the subject matter with which political science deals admits of adequate understanding in terms of "laws," or whether the universals through which political things can be understood as what they are must not be conceived of in entirely different terms. Scientific concern with political facts, relations of political facts, recurrent relations of political facts, or laws of political behavior requires isolation of the phenomena which it is studying. But if this isolation is not to lead to irrelevant or misleading results, one must see the phenomena in question within the whole to which they belong, and one must clarify that whole; i.e., the whole political or politico-social order: e.g., one cannot arrive at a kind of knowledge, which deserves to be called scientific, of "group politics," if one does not reflect on what genus of political orders is presupposed if there is to be "group politics" at all, and what kind of political order is presupposed by the specific "group politics" which one is studying. But one cannot clarify the character of a specific democracy, or of democracy in general, without having a clear understanding of the alternatives to democracy. Scientific political scientists are inclined to leave it at the distinction between democracy and authoritarianism; i.e., they absolutize the given political order by remaining within a horizon which is defined by the given political order and its opposite. The scientific approach tends to lead to the neglect of the primary or fundamental questions and therewith to thoughtless acceptance of received opinion. As regards these fundamental questions our friends of scientific exactness are strangely unexacting. To refer again to the most simple and at the same time decisive example, political science requires clarification of what distinguishes political things from things which are not political; it requires that the question be raised and answered "what is political?" This question cannot be dealt with scientifically but only dialectically. And dialectical treatment necessarily begins from prescientific knowledge and takes it most seriously. Prescientific knowledge, or "common sense" knowledge, is thought to be discredited by Copernicus and the succeeding natural science. But the fact that what we may call telescopic-microscopic knowledge is very fruitful in certain areas, does not entitle one to deny that there are things which can only be seen as what they are, if they are seen with the unarmed eye; or more precisely, if they are seen in the perspective of the citizen, as distinguished from the perspective of the scientific observer. If one denies this, one will repeat the experience of Gulliver with the nurse in Brobdingnag and become entangled in the kind of research projects by which he was amazed in Laputa.

4. Positivism necessarily transforms itself into historicism. By virtue of its orientation by the model of natural science, social science is in danger of mistaking peculiarities of, say, mid-twentieth-century United States, or more generally of modern Western society, for the essential character of human society. To avoid this danger, it is compelled to engage in "cross-cultural research," in the study of other cultures, both present and past. But in making this effort, it misses the meaning of those other cultures, because it interprets them through a conceptual scheme which originates in modern Western society, which reflects that particular society, and which fits at best only that particular society. To avoid this danger, social science must attempt to understand those cultures as they understand or understood themselves: the understanding primarily required of the social scientist is historical understanding. Historical understanding becomes the basis of a truly empirical science of society. But if one considers the infinity of the task of historical understanding, one begins to wonder whether historical understanding does

not take the place of the scientific study of society. Furthermore, social science is said to be a body of true propositions about social phenomena. The propositions are answers to questions. What valid answers—objectively valid answers— are, may be determined by the rules or principles of logic. But the questions depend on one's direction of interest, and hence on one's values; i.e., on subjective principles. Now it is the direction of interests, and not logic, which supplies the fundamental concepts. It is therefore not possible to divorce from each other the subjective and objective elements of social science; the objective answers receive their meaning from the subjective questions. If one does not relapse into the decayed Platonism which is underlying the notion of timeless values, one must conceive of the values embodied in a given social science as dependent on the society to which the social science in question belongs; i.e., on history. Not only is social science superseded by historical studies; social science itself proves to be "historical." Reflection on social science as a historical phenomenon leads to the relativization of social science and ultimately of modern science generally. As a consequence, modern science comes to be viewed as one historically relative way of understanding things which is not in principle superior to alternative ways of understanding.

It is only at this point that we come face to face with the serious antagonist of political philosophy: historicism. After having reached its full growth historicism is distinguished from positivism by the following characteristics. (1) It abandons the distinction between facts and values, because every understanding, however theoretical, implies specific evaluations. (2) It denies the authoritative character of modern science, which appears as only one among the many forms of man's intellectual orientation in the world. (3) It refuses to regard the historical process as fundamentally progressive, or, more generally stated, as reasonable. (4) It denies the relevance of the evolutionist thesis by contending that the evolution of man out of non-man cannot make intelligible man's humanity. Historicism rejects the question of the good society, that is to say, of *the* good society because of the essentially historical character of society and of human thought: there is no essential necessity for raising the question of the good society; this question is not in principle coeval with man; its very possibility is the outcome of a mysterious dispensation of fate. The crucial issue concerns the status of those permanent characteristics of humanity, such as the distinction between the noble and the base, which are admitted by the thoughtful historicists: can these permanencies be used as criteria for distinguishing between good and bad dispensations of fate? The historicist answers this question in the negative. He looks down on the permanencies in question because of their objective, common, superficial and rudimentary character: to become relevant, they would have to be completed, and their completion is no longer common but historical. It was the contempt for these permanencies which permitted the most radical historicist in 1933 to submit to, or rather to welcome, as a dispensation of fate, the verdict of the least wise and least moderate part of his nation while it was in its least wise and least moderate mood, and at the same time to speak of wisdom and moderation. The events of 1933 would rather seem to have proved, if such proof was necessary, that man cannot abandon the question of the good society, and that he cannot free himself from the responsibility for answering it by deferring to history or to any other power different from his own reason.

5 : *Politics and Pseudopolitics: A Critical Evaluation of Some Behavioral Literature*

CHRISTIAN BAY

A curious state of affairs has developed within the academic discipline that bravely calls itself Political Science—the discipline that in a much-quoted phrase has been called "a device, invented by university teachers, for avoiding that dangerous subject, politics, without achieving science."[1] A growing and now indeed a predominant proportion of leading American political scientists, the behavioralists, have become determined to achieve science. Yet in the process many of them remain open to the charge of strenuously avoiding that dangerous subject, politics.

Consider a recent essay on the behavioral persuasion in politics. The conclusion stresses the purpose of political

Reprinted from *American Political Science Review*, 59 (March 1965), 39–51, by permission of the author and the publisher. The author acknowledges "my friend Herbert H. Hyman, who has been generous with advice for improvements on an earlier draft. It should not be inferred that he is in agreement with opinions expressed in this paper, or that he might not once again find much to criticize in it. At a later stage I have received helpful suggestions also from Sidney Verba and Andrew Hacker."

inquiry: "The Goal is Man." There is to be a commitment to some humane purpose after all. But what kind of man? A democratic kind of man, a just man, or perhaps a power-seeking man? The answer follows: "These are philosophical questions better left to the philosophers."[2] Behavioral students of politics should, as scientists, engage in no value judgments concerning the kind of man or society their researches ought to serve. This is the general inference to be drawn, not only from this particular essay, but from much of the contemporary literature on political behavior.

As Heinz Eulau, the author, points out in the same essay, the area of behavioral political science includes a particular domain called policy science, in which empirical inquiry is geared to explicitly stated goal formulations; within *this* domain "political science, as all science, should be put in the service of whatever goals men pursue in politics." *Any* goals? Not quite; in this context Eulau points out that the choice of what goals to serve is a matter of personal ethics, and incidentally reminds us that behavioral research can be readily utilized also for purposes conflicting with the original ones. "In this sense, at least, science is value-free. I don't think the scientist can escape this dilemma of having his work misused without giving up his calling." And the author concludes with these words: "Only if he places himself at the service of those whose values he disagrees with does he commit intellectual treason."

In these pages I am concerned with sins less serious than intellectual treason; perhaps intellectual indolence is a more accurate term. My argument will be that much of the current work on political behavior generally fails to articulate its very real value biases, and that the political impact of this supposedly neutral literature is generally conservative and in a special sense anti-political. In conclusion I propose to develop a perspective on political inquiry that would relate it more meaningfully to problems of human needs and values; in that context I will suggest some important but neglected problems lending themselves to empirical research.

I am not about to argue that our investments in political behavior research have been too large; on the contrary, we need much more work in this area. But my principal concern is to argue for a more pressing need: an intellectually more defensible and a politically more responsible theoretical framework for guiding and interpreting our empirical work; a theory that would give more meaning to our research, even at the expense of reducing its conceptual and operational neatness.

I

It is necessary first to clarify some basic terms in which my concern is stated.

The prevailing concepts of "politics" in the literature under consideration are surely an important source of the difficulty. Definitions gravitate toward the most conspicuous *facts* and shy away from all reference to more norm-laden and less easily measurable aspects of social life. For the sake of brevity, let us consider only the most recent formulation by one of the unquestionably most influential political scientists of the present generation: "A political system is any persistent pattern of human relationships that involves, to a significant extent, power, rule, or authority."[3] My objection is not primarily to the extension of the reference of "political" to private as well as to public associations, and even to clans and families as well; rather, it is to the absence of any reference to a public purpose. Research work on power, rule, or authority can contribute significantly to our political knowledge, even if the data come from contexts not ordinarily thought of as political. But its significance must be gauged in relation to some criteria; until these are articulated and justified, or at any rate chosen, we can only intuit whether our researches on, say, power behavior are tackling significant or trivial issues.

"Politics" should refer to power, but the term should

also refer to some conception of human welfare or the public good. The achievement of Plato and Aristotle is in part a result of their starting out by asking some of the right questions; above all, what is politics *for?* Their limitations were logical and methodological or, if you prefer, conceptual: they had not learned to distinguish between verifiable *descriptive* statements, statements of *normative* positions, and (empirically empty and normatively neutral) *analytical* statements, including definitions and other equations.

Once these distinctions had been developed, a process that began with David Hume, it became easy and fashionable to expose fallacies in Plato and Aristotle; but instead of attacking the ancient and perennial problems of politics with our new and sharper conceptual tools, recent generations of political scientists appear to have sought safety in seeking to exclude the normative realm altogether from the scope of their scientific inquiry. "Politics" has consequently been defined in a simple institutional or behavioral manner, unrelated to normative conceptions of any sort. Ironically, most modern behavioralists are back with the Greeks again in their assumption that political inquiry can be pursued by much the same methods as natural science inquiry; they have adjusted to David Hume and the modern logical positivists by the neat device of definitions that limit the scope of their inquiry to observable behavior.

This surely is a stance of premature closure. The alternative proposed here is to insist on the need for a political theory that deals with *basic human needs* as well as overt desires and other observable aspects of behavior. The task of improving concepts and methods toward establishing a stricter science of politics is formidable; but let us avoid establishing an orthodoxy that would have the whole profession contract for a fainthearted purchase of rigor at the price of excluding much of the meat and spirit of politics.

As a modest and fragmentary beginning toward a more appropriate theory, let me suggest a distinction between "politics" and "pseudopolitics." I would define as *political* all activity aimed at improving or protecting conditions for the satisfaction of human needs and demands in a given society or community, according to some universalistic scheme of priorities, implicit or explicit.[4] *Pseudopolitical* in this paper refers to activity that resembles political activity but is exclusively concerned with either the alleviation of personal neuroses or with promoting private or private interest-group advantage, deterred by no articulate or disinterested conception of what would be just or fair to other groups.

Pseudopolitics is the counterfeit of politics. The relative prevalence of the counterfeit variety of democratic politics presumably depends on many ascertainable factors, including a society's degree of commercialization and the degree of socioeconomic mobility (or the size of the stakes in the competitive struggle); on the other hand, the proportion of pseudopolitical activity would correlate negatively with the amount of psychological security, the amount of social welfare-type security, and the amount of political education effectively taught.

For present purposes it is not necessary to demonstrate in detail how the distinction between politics in the narrower sense and pseudopolitics can be made operationally useful. Suffice it to say that only a saint is pure from the taint of pseudopolitics and that hardly any pseudopolitician would be *wholly* without concern for the public welfare; mixed motives, in proportions varying from one person to the next and from one situation to the next, pervade all actions. It is a difficult but surely not an impossible task to develop indices for assessing the relative prevalence of political versus pseudopolitical incentives in voters and other political actors; the only essential prerequisite is to decide that the task must be tackled.

Without attempting to make this kind of distinction, untidy as it may at first appear to many a behavioralist, I don't see how we can begin to approach a condition of tidiness in our discussions of the *political significance* of research, or of the *political responsibility* of political scientists. But what should we mean by these two highly eulogistic terms; might we not be better advised to shun them altogether? The bulk of this paper seeks to demonstrate some sorry consequences of the latter course. We cannot avoid the realm of normative issues unless we really wish to disclaim all political significance for our work. Probably very few in our profession would adopt this position.

Although explicit cognizance of normative assumptions in his theoretical frame of reference is likely to entail some inconvenience for the researcher, he will by no means be blocked from continuing much of his present work. It should be clear that all competent research on pseudopolitical behavior illuminates political behavior as well as the relative presence of one signals the relative absence of the other. In the real world the two aspects of behavior always coexist. My quarrel is not with research on pseudopolitics per se, but with the way findings are usually reported and interpreted. I object to the tendency in much of the behavior literature to deal with the pseudopolitical aspects of behavior almost exclusively, and to imply that the prevalence of pseudopolitics is and always will be the natural or even the desirable state of affairs in a democracy. Consequently, I object also to the absence of interest in research that could reveal some of the determinants of the relative prevalence of pseudopolitical behavior on our political arena, by which we might learn more about how we may advance toward a more strictly political consciousness, in the sense of concern for the public interest and for the future, in our profession.

Now, how should we define political significance and political responsibility? In my conceptual world the two terms are tied together; I would judge degrees of political significance of research studies in the same way that I would judge degrees of political responsibility of political scientists (in the role of theorist-researcher, as distinct from the role of citizen). A research report is politically significant to the extent that it contributes to the kinds of knowledge most needed by politically responsible political scientists.

"Political responsibility" in this paper refers to the extent to which the social scientist observes the canons of rationality on two levels, which I shall call formal and substantive.[5] Formal rationality refers to the familiar notion of clarifying the objectives first and then paying heed to the best available knowledge when seeking ways and means to implement them. Competent behavioral research in political science is highly rational in this formal sense; this is what the extensive work in theory and methodology is *for*.

The lack of political responsibility that I ascribe to much political behavior literature relates to the other level of rationality, the substantive level, which involves articulate attention to questions of fundamental commitment in social and political research literature. Problems of human welfare (including justice, liberty, security, etc.), the objects of political research and of politics, can be adequately studied, and dealt with, only if their *ought*-side is investigated as carefully as their *is*-side. Ought-side inquiry must pertain to wants (or desires or, if insisted on, demands) as well as needs. Political communication must be analyzed carefully so that we may learn what aspects of *wants* are most salient and could be frustrated only at the cost of resentment, alienation, or upheaval. Yet, only analysis of data on wants in terms of a theory of *needs* will permit us to evaluate wants and aspects of wants with a view to longer-term consequences of their relative satisfaction or frustration.

There will be more to say about wants and needs in the concluding section. At this point it should only be added that the student of politics, once he has adopted a conception of human needs, should proceed from there to make explicit his inferences about political objectives and his choice of commitments with the utmost care. If this kind of inquiry is neglected, as it certainly is in the political science curricula in most of our universities, the danger is that the political scientist unwittingly becomes the tool of other people's commitments. And *theirs* may be even less responsibly arrived at; conceivably, the expertise of the political scientist may come to serve the irrational purposes of genteel bigotry in domestic policies or of paranoid jingoism and reckless gambling with our chances of survival in foreign policies. If advice-giving social scientists don't feel called on to invest their best intellectual energies in studying the ultimate ends of our national policies, it is unlikely that anyone else of influence will; most active politicians have, after all, more immediately pressing worries, and all these are anyway the kinds of concerns they are best trained to handle.

Intellectual treason, to return to Eulau's phrase, is probably a remote hazard in our profession. For, rather than placing himself in the service "of those whose values he disagrees with," the political scientist usually will by natural, uninvestigated processes come to agree with the prevailing values of his profession, of the major foundations and of his government, at least on the more basic public policy objectives and assumptions. His training and career incentives focus on formal rationality. It is fortunate that many social scientists for other reasons tend to be humane and liberal individuals. We will be far better off, however, if we can make it respectable or even mandatory for many more of our researchers to be guided in their choice of theory and problems by their own articulated values, instead of acting willy-nilly on the supposedly neutral values impressed on them by the conventional wisdom of their profession.

II

In the contemporary political science literature it is by no means unusual to see the articulation of political norms begin and end with a commitment to "democracy" in some unspecified sense. Fifteen years ago a respected political scientist suggested a more critical orientation: "The democratic myth is that the people are inherently wise and just, and that they are the real rulers of the republic. These propositions do have meaning; but if they become, as they do even among scholars, matters of faith, then scientific progress has been sacrificed in the interest of a morally satisfying demagogy."[6] This advice has not been generally heeded. Even today many political scientists are writing as if democracy unquestionably is a good thing, from which unquestionably good things will flow, while at the same time they profess a disinterest in settling value issues. "The only cure for the ills of democracy is more democracy" is still the implicit slogan of quite a few social scientists, who seem unaware of even the *conceptual* difficulties involved in developing generally useful criteria, let alone a rationale, for "more democracy." To put it bluntly, it appears that a good number of otherwise able political scientists confuse a vaguely stated conventional "democratism"[7] with scientific objectivity.

That behavioral research not explicitly related to problems of democracy tends to be vague in its implications for normative democratic theory is perhaps to be expected. It is paradoxical that some of the leading behavioral writers *on democracy* continue to write as if they want to have it both ways: to be rigorously value-neutral and at the same time be impeccable champions of conventional pluralist democracy. To straddle on a sharp issue would not be comfortable; if we want to write as good democrats and as logical positivists too, it is perhaps necessary to be obtuse on issues like "why democracy?" or "what is democracy for?" and, indeed, "what is democracy?"

For a first example, take the late V. O. Key's most recent book on *Public Opinion and American Democracy*.[8] Here we are presented with an admirably organized survey of what is now known of the characteristics of contemporary public opinion and of the extent of its bearing on American governmental decision processes. Yet for all these facts about public opinion, there is hardly a hint of their implications, in the author's judgment, for any of the relevant normative issues of democracy; what little is said on this score is uninformative indeed. For example, the point is made toward the end that political deviants "play a critical role in the preservation of the vitality of a democratic order as they urge alterations and modifications better to achieve the aspirations of men. Hence the fundamental significance of freedom of speech and agitation" (p. 555). There is no elaboration of this point, which one might take to be an important issue, considering the book's title and general subject. And there is no other discussion of what purpose all this political knowledge should serve. Is it the "preservation of the vitality of a democratic order" as far as we can articulate the criteria for the best possible government, or for trends in the best direction? What does "vitality" mean here, and what aspects of our democracy are most in need of it? Is free speech valuable solely as a means to this rather obscurely conceived end?

Or take the volume on *Voting* by a team of top-notch political sociologists.[9] One of the book's two themes, we are told (p. x), is the social problem of how political preferences are formed, while the "confrontation of democratic theory with democratic practice is the second implied theme that runs throughout the book." There is much about certain kinds of practices, yes; but democratic theory is limited to a few examples of "impossible" demands of "traditional normative theory" on the role of the citizen: that he should be politically interested, knowledgeable and rational. These investigators find that most voters are indeed politically apathetic, ignorant and far from rational in their political behavior.

Given the second theme one might have expected the authors to raise some pertinent questions concerning the sense, if any, in which we nevertheless do have a democracy, or possibly the sense in which we nevertheless *ought* to be able to have a democracy, if what we have now does not fit this concept. Or perhaps an attempt toward reformulating democratic norms in better accord with political realities, if the term "democracy" should be saved for new uses.

Nothing of the sort happens. Instead, the authors make the happy discovery that the *system of democracy* that we have "does meet certain requirements for a going political organization"; indeed, as it is said just before, "it often works with distinction" (p. 312). What is good and bad about the system is left in the dark, as is the question of criteria for "distinction." Instead, we are given a list of dimensions of citizen behavior, and are told that the fact that individuals differ on these various dimensions (e.g., involvement—indifference) somehow is exactly what the modern democratic system requires. It all ends well, then; and in parting the authors leave us with this comforting if question-begging assurance: "Twentieth-century political theory—both analytic and *normative*—will arise *only* from hard and long observation of the actual world of politics, closely identified with the deeper problems of practical politics." (p. 323. Italics supplied.) *Only?*

Turn now to a widely and deservedly praised book with the promising title, *A Preface to Democratic Theory*. Robert Dahl explains his choice of title by asserting that "there is no democratic theory—only democratic theories. This fact suggests that we had better proceed by considering some representative theories in order to discover what kinds of problems they raise. . . ."[10] And in the landscape of behavioral literature this work does stand out as an impressive exercise in logical analysis. Excellent critical evaluations of the Madisonian and the populist-type democratic theories are offered; but subsequently Dahl changes his tack to what he calls (p. 63) the descriptive method: under "polyarchal democracy" he seeks to develop empirical criteria for a concept of democracy based on our knowledge of existing species. As we would expect of a competent behavioralist, the author develops some enlightening perspectives on how "the American hybrid" in fact appears to be functioning.

Penetrating as this account of the basic operating procedures of the American democracy is, the author's criteria for evaluating the result are surprisingly inarticulate and *ad hoc*. He will *not* try to determine whether it is a desirable system of government, he assures us toward the end of the book; and then proceeds to do just that, but vaguely:

> . . . It appears to be a relatively efficient system for reinforcing agreement, encouraging moderation, and maintaining social peace in a restless and immoderate people operating a gigantic, powerful, diversified, and incredibly complex society. This is no negligible contribution, then, that Americans have made to the arts of government—and to that branch, which of all the arts of politics is the most difficult, the art of democratic government.

These are Dahl's parting words.

Having subjected the assumptions, hypotheses, implied definitions, and even the presumed value axioms of two theories of democracy to painstaking analysis, the author's ambition not to discuss the desirability of the American system of government would be difficult to understand for someone unacquainted with the currently prevailing fashions among behavioralists. To study the definitional characteristics of this hybrid species of government and of the genus, "polyarchal democracy," is a worthwhile endeavor, to be sure, but would in my opinion assume far greater significance if pursued within a framework of value assumptions, however tentatively presented, from which could be derived operational criteria for judging what aspects of a functioning democracy ought to be valued and strengthened, as against other aspects that should be deplored and, if possible, counteracted. Why does the author never say clearly whether in *his* view democracy is something to be valued in itself, and maximized (as he takes Madisonian theory to assert), or as valuable for some specified ends (for example, for maximizing political equality, after the fashion of populists)?

In a Preface to democratic theory, and one which demonstrates a high order of rigor in analyzing other theories of democracy, the author's reluctance even to begin to develop operating criteria toward making meaningful the present system, or to provide pointers toward its more meaningful further development, is as astounding as it is disappointing. Reluctantly one concludes that Dahl in this particular context behaves like most political behavioralists: he feels he can permit himself to write normatively about political purposes, it would seem, only if they are stated in terms of "democracy" and are reasonably indeterminate, lest the suspicion should arise that he is pleading for some politically partisan position. Thus, a demeanor of scientific objectivity is maintained, and so is a persistently implied commitment to a certain political bias, which favors democracy roughly as it now exists in the West, or in this country.

III

Leo Strauss charges the behavioralists with a bias toward liberal democracy, and rightly so, in comparison to his position. Yet in some respects the bias of much behavioralist political literature is profoundly conservative, although this is a species of conservatism rather different from Strauss'. Philosophically speaking, this behaviorally oriented conservatism frequently includes an *anti-political* dimension which is not found in Strauss' work.[11] What is anti-political is the assumption, explicit or implicit, that politics, or at any rate American politics, is and must always remain primarily a system of rules for peaceful battles between competing private interests, and not an arena for the struggle toward a more humane and more rationally organized society.

Consider S. M. Lipset's recent suggestion that the age-old

search for the good society can be terminated, for we have got it now. Democracy as we know it "is the good society itself in operation." Not that our democracy cannot still be improved upon, but roughly speaking, it appears, "the give-and-take of a free society's internal struggles" is the best that men can hope for. Our society is so good that Lipset welcomes, at least for the West, what he sees as a trend toward replacing political ideology with sociological analysis.[12]

This is an extreme statement, although by a leading and deservedly famous political sociologist. We cannot saddle behavioralists in general with responsibility for such phrasing. But in substance, as we shall see, the same tendency toward affirming the status quo and, what is worse, toward disclaiming the importance and even the legitimacy of political ideology, and ideals, is discernible in other leading behaviorally oriented works as well.

Let us note incidentally that all the behavioral works referred to so far wind up affirming that American democracy on the whole works well, while failing to articulate the criteria on which this judgment is based.[13] In fairness it should be added that probably all these writers would make an exception for the place of the Negro and certain other underprivileged groups or categories for whom our democracy admittedly does not work so well; there are flaws, then, but fundamentally all is well or else will become well without any basic changes.

What is more troublesome than this somewhat conservative commitment to a somewhat liberal conception of democracy[14] —whether acknowledged or surreptitious—is the antipolitical orientation referred to a moment ago; the failure to see politics as potentially, at least, an instrument of reason, legitimately dedicated to the improvement of social conditions.

Within a brief space that allows no extensive documentation perhaps the next best thing to do is to consider for a moment a recent example of a behavioralist approach in which, for a change, the underlying assumptions are spelled out with commendable clarity, and then let the reader judge to what extent other literature referred to above may not implicitly rest on similar starkly antipolitical premises.

James M. Buchanan and Gordon Tullock have called their book *The Calculus of Consent,* with subtitle *Logical Foundations of Constitutional Democracy.*[15] The task set for the book, we are told in the Preface, is "to analyze the calculus of the rational individual when he is faced with questions of constitutional choice"; the authors, both of whom have most of their training in economics, intend to develop what they take to be the rationale for group action in the public sector in a free society—i.e., for political action.

The authors take pains to assert the value-free nature of their approach to the science of politics. True, they choose to go along with "the Western philosophical tradition" in so far as they consider the human individual "the primary philosophical entity" (p. 11). From here on, supposedly, we are dealing with the political processes that flow from the desire of all individuals to try to maximize whatever they may value. "The grail-like search for some 'public interest' apart from, and independent of, the separate interests of the individual participants in social choice" (p. 12) is not the concern of *these* authors.

Only in one limited sense do the authors recognize a sort of collective interest in a free society: "it is rational to *have a constitution*" (p. 21), or a set of rules for deciding how decisions in the public sector are to be arrived at; *constitutional* issues are in principle to be settled by unanimity, while *operational* issues—all other political issues—must be settled according to constitutional provisions. The authors see no rationale for majoritarianism as a way of deciding, unless a constitution happens to require it in given contexts; consequently, constitutions can be changed only by unanimity, according to this "individualistic theory of political process," as one of the authors has lately named the theory.[16]

In his more recent statement, Buchanan recognizes as an "entirely reasonable interpretation" (p. 7) that this approach to political processes can be seen as a model for the defense of the status quo. His most important rejoinder is that "analysis must start from somewhere, and the existing set of rules and institutions is the only place from which it is possible to start" (p. 7).

The previously cited writings of leading behavioralists have been less explicit and also less bold in showing the way from assertedly value-free premises toward a conservative and in my sense anti-political orientation. Yet, in all the works given critical attention above, there are normative ambiguities wide enough to make room for a theory such as the one offered by Buchanan and Tullock. This is not to say that Eulau, Key, Berelson *et al.*, Dahl, or Lipset would concur with Buchanan and Tullock in their normative position. But their approach to politics is philosophically similar in its emphasis on prevailing behavior patterns here and now as the thing to study and in its rejection of the legitimacy of normative positions as frameworks for research (except in a normatively *ad hoc* policy science context). Buchanan and Tullock have been able to explicate in considerable detail *one* rationale for an implicit stance that appears to be widely shared by students of politics today.

If a similar orientation were to be adopted in medical literature, its scope would in the main be confined to studying how patients choose to cope or at any rate do cope with their pathologies, while omitting or neglecting fundamental study of conditions for possible treatment and prevention.

IV

Unlike other behavioral literature, modern works in comparative politics almost always focus on real political problems; when political institutions are compared cross-nationally or cross-culturally, pseudopolitical behavior can more readily be seen as dysfunctional in terms of some conception or other of the public good; usually such conceptions are couched in terms of "'modernization" or "development," at least if comparisons are cross-cultural as well as cross-national. The point is that developmental perspectives and therefore political purposes are ever-present in this literature, even if they are not often well articulated. Yet, what is particularly impressive in some of this literature is its conceptual and theoretical scope, including the stress on psychological as well as social component explanations of political behavior, and on the need for integrating micro-analyses of large collectivities.[17]

Concerned as the modern students of comparative politics have been with substantive problems, they have resisted temptations to pursue their inquiries according to immediately practical considerations such as the availability of operational indices and techniques of measurement.[18] On the contrary, insistent efforts have been made to innovate concepts that would take account of variables which are not as yet accessible to observation and quantification—concepts such as political culture, political socialization, political identity, and political style, for example. The long-term strategy appears to be to start out with concepts broad enough to encompass all significant aspects of political reality, and then work toward parceling out component concepts which come closer to corresponding to variables that can be observed, perhaps indirectly and by tentative indices at first. Thus the theoretical working hypotheses can gradually, it is hoped, be subjected to increasingly direct and stringent tests. This is a far cry from the piecemeal approach to political (or pseudopolitical) reality in many other works, which almost exclusively pays attention to disparate empirical relationships while neglecting to consider the possible systematic-theoretical reasons we might have for taking an interest in them.

There is also this to be said about the modern comparative politics literature, however, that its conceptual and theoretical innovations have as yet failed to make a significant dent in the same democratic myth that Almond himself —the leader in this field—has warned us against years ago (above, p. 117). The dilemma already discussed, of desiring to support democracy and adopt a stance of value neutrality too, has not as yet been satisfactorily resolved in this literature either. And this failure is paradoxical in this particular context, in part because the ostensible chief concern is with "development" or "modernization" as the dependent variable, so that the question of development toward *what* immediately suggests itself. The failure is paradoxical also because these scholars have coined bold new concepts on the independent side of the ledger, and some have written extensively about concepts as far removed from realms of observation as "political culture" and "political identity."[19] Yet a concept such as "human need" has not been touched, and discussions of key terms like "political development" or "modernization" have been hampered, it would seem, by an unwillingness to question whether democratic ways or what kinds of democratic ways are most conductive to satisfying human needs.[20]

In the most extensive recent discussion of these concepts La Palombara begins well with a warning that what many scholars appear to have in mind "when they speak of a modern or developed system is one that approximates the institutional and structural configuration that we associate with the Anglo-American (in any event, the Western) democratic systems" (p. 10). He calls this conceptualization culture-bound; yet in the same and the following chapter he goes to considerable lengths himself in arguing for the use of the same kinds of culture-bound criteria to evaluate development or modernity abroad. While he contributes a useful discussion of different dimensions along which political change can be measured, he never inquires whether in other countries there might be other criteria of development of equal or greater significance than his own essentially Anglo-Saxon criteria. "One of the great dilemmas of many of the developing countries," he writes, "is that they seem to want economic development more than freedom" (p. 41), and the last term he takes as a matter of course to refer to pluralist institutions. "Why should it not be possible to raise a belief in and desire for democracy to the same level?" (p. 58). And in conclusion La Palombara asserts that we Americans must expand our efforts to export not only technical know-how "but our political ideology and reasonable facsimiles of our political institutions and practices as well." Without such an effort, he adds, he is reasonably confident that "the probability of attaining democratic configuration in most of the newer states is very low indeed" (pp. 60–61).

The main difficulty with this reasoning is that men are motivated, also politically, by their immediate needs and wants, and not by foreign orthodoxies. La Palombara speculates "whether it would not be possible to manipulate demands so that goals of political development enjoy a status equal to that of economic change" (p. 30), and suggests the encouragement of private as against collectively oriented enterprise for this end. The answer is surely a flat no: it is *not* possible, in most countries in which most people are economically underprivileged, to create a broad popular interest in pluralist democratic institutions. "Acceptance of the norms of democracy requires a high level of sophistication and ego security," writes Lipset, on the basis of a variety of loosely connected empirical data.[21] An active concern for the public welfare presupposes a liberation both from anxiety neuroses and from realistic fears concerning one's own and one's family's physical sustenance, welfare and security. To put it more succinctly, needs for food and safety take precedence over political interest; no amount of political manipulation could be expected to alter such priorities.

To be sure, individuals can be lured into "the game of politics" as advantageous careers under the right circumstances; but is this the kind of political development that the West should desire? If budding Western–democracy-type pluralist institutions turn out to benefit only the middle and upper classes—as in many Latin American countries—then we should not be surprised if idealistic students and others with a passion for social justice, or for politics as distinct from pseudopolitics, may become disposed to reject the forms of pluralist democracy altogether.[22]

Nevertheless, the trend among political behavioralists, including students of comparative politics, appears to be toward a clean break not only with Plato's concern with justice as something above democracy, for the true philosopher; also, it seems that the classical conception of democracy as a system of rational deliberation for settling issues of justice and welfare is on its way out, *even as a political ideal*. Reference has been made to the *ad hoc* attempts of Berelson *et al.* to bring the norms of democracy in better accord with the facts of what I have termed pseudopolitical behavior. In *The Civic Culture* Almond and Verba present and discuss a variety of usefully differentiated survey data collected in five countries (United States, Britain, West Germany, Italy and Mexico). "What we have done in this book," they conclude, "is to spell out methodically the mixture of attitudes that support a democratic system. If it can create a more sober and informed appreciation of the nature and complexity of the problems of democratization, it will have served its purpose."[23] But what kind of democracy? The theoretical point of departure is neither in a conception of human needs nor in the classical theories of democracy, but in such literature as has been discussed above—notably Dahl's *Preface to Democratic Theory* and the last chapter in Berelson's *Voting*. In fact, Almond and Verba emphatically reject the classical "rationality-activist" ideal of democratic citizenship in favor of a more balanced "parochial-subject-participant" orientation; in a healthy, stable democracy as they conceive it (and American political culture comes close even though it does not quite embody this ideal), "the democratic citizen is called on to pursue contradictory goals; he must be active, yet passive; involved, yet not too involved; influential, yet deferential."[24]

Perhaps so, if the ultimate goal is democratic stability. And there is no denying, from my normative position, that democratic stability is valuable, and that many nations ought to have more of it. But is it the most important goal for political development; is it the goal that should serve as the basis for evaluating all other goals (whether wholly, in terms of instrumentality, or partially, in terms of compatibility)? Should we not instead hold, in Eulau's phrase, that "The Goal is Man"?

V

In the study of political behavior, "analysis must start from somewhere, and the existing set of rules and institutions is the only place from which it is possible to start," according to Buchanan. Students of comparative politics have nevertheless demonstrated the feasibility of analyzing political developments in some countries in terms of valuable outcomes achieved in others.[25] It remains to be shown that political behavior and institutions can be analyzed also in terms of normative assumptions to the effect that the purpose of politics is to meet human needs and facilitate human development.

Contrary to an apparently prevailing assumption among political behavioralists, psychological phenomena are just as *real* as economic and voting behavior phenomena, even though admittedly less accessible to observation and measurement. Some more of the same conceptual boldness displayed in the recent literature on comparative politics is required if political inquiry is to become related to important human wants and needs. For one thing, we need to distinguish more clearly between pseudopolitical and more strictly political behavior, if we want to learn how to encourage the latter at the expense of the former.[26]

A major conceptual and theoretical task is to develop a satisfactory theory of human needs and of the relationships between needs and *wants*—here referring to perceived or felt needs. Wants (or, synonymously, desires) and demands can be observed and measured by way of asking people or observing their behavior. Needs, on the other hand, can only be inferred from their hypothetical consequences for behavior or, more manifestly, from the actual consequences of their frustration. Whenever superficial wants are fulfilled but underlying needs remain frustrated, pathological behavior is likely to ensue.

Prior to the development of a viable theory of political development is at least a beginning toward a theory of individual human development. Such a beginning exists in psychological literature, but it has so far been inadequately drawn on by students of political behavior. Let me very briefly suggest the direction of this theorizing, and some of its implications for the study of political behavior.

Basic human needs are characteristics of the human organism, and they are presumably less subject to change than the social or even the physical conditions under which men live. Wants are sometimes manifestations of real needs, but, as Plato and many other wise men since have insisted, we cannot always infer the existence of needs from wants. Wants are often artificially induced by outside manipulation, or they may be neurotically based desires whose satisfaction fails to satisfy needs, or both. Emphasis on a civic-culture type of democracy as the goal for political development may well perpetuate a state of affairs in which human needs as seen by the political minded (in my strict sense of "political") will remain in the shadow of much-advertised human

wants as promoted by pseudopoliticians and other enter-
prisers whose horizons do not extend beyond their own
occupational or career interests and status anxieties.[27]

I say *may*, for I am raising a question rather than adopting
a position. In order to investigate the relationship between
needs and wants as they pertain to political functions we
must start out with a tentative conception of priorities among
human needs. The best available point of departure, in my
opinion, is in A. H. Maslow's theory of a hierarchy of human needs; this theorizing ought to be drawn on until a
more plausible and useful theory becomes available.

Maslow lists five categories of needs in the order of their
assumed priority: (1) physical needs (air, water, food, etc.);
(2) safety needs (assurance of survival and of continuing
satisfaction of basic needs); (3) needs to love and be loved;
(4) need for esteem (by self and others); and (5) need for
self-actualization and growth. This list presents a hierarchy,
according to Maslow, in the sense that the "less prepotent
needs are minimized, even forgotten or denied. But when
a need is fairly well satisfied, the next prepotent ('higher')
need emerges, in turn to dominate the conscious life and
to serve as the center of organization of behavior, since
gratified needs are not active motivators."[28] Note, however,
that whenever in the course of a human life the "higher"
needs have become activated, they are not necessarily ex-
tinguished as a result of later deprivation of "lower" or more
basic needs. For example, some individuals, provided they
have once known physical safety, will unhesitatingly sacri-
fice all of it for love, or for standards of right conduct tied
in with their self-esteem, etc.

In a recent volume, James C. Davies has suggested the
utility of Maslow's theory as a generator of propositions regarding political behavior, and he illustrates the plausibility
(without demonstrating the validity) of such propositions with
a wealth of historical and contemporary political behavior
data. For example, according to Davies's theorizing it is

impractical to suggest, with La Palombara, that it might be "possible to manipulate demands" in economically under-developed countries so that widespread loyalties to democratic institutions could emerge: "Long before there can be responsible or irresponsible popular government, long before the question of dictatorship or democracy can be taken up, the problem of survival must be solved so that a political community itself can develop, so that people can direct some of their attention to politics."[29] In another context he says, "Propaganda cannot paint a picture which conflicts with reality as it is seen by individuals in the light of their basic needs" (p. 134); the picture can be painted all right, but it will be a wasted effort. And Davies quotes Kwame Nkrumah, whose implicit rejoinder to La Palombara's argument is hard to improve on: "We cannot tell our peoples that material benefits in growth and modern progress are not for them. If we do, they will throw us out and seek other leaders who promise more. . . . We have to modernize. Either we shall do so with the interest and support of the West or we shall be compelled to turn elsewhere. This is not a warning or a threat, but a straight statement of political reality" (p. 135).

One shortcoming in Davies's as well as Maslow's work, in my judgment, is that both authors seek to relate events and behavior directly to the elusive concept of "need," without the use of an intermediate and more manageable concept such as "want." Both concepts are badly needed, and their interrelations and their application in hypotheses must be developed if we want to move toward a more adequate knowledge of political behavior. It must be granted that manifest wants are important aspects of our political reality, especially in democracies; what matters is that we also keep remembering, unlike many behavioralists, that there also are genuine needs to worry about, elusive though they may be to the researcher's conventional tools. The volume of competing loudspeakers, if I may use a metaphor, is in a pluralist democracy perhaps more likely to depend on the power of the purse than on the urgency of the need. Even the most democratic governments are likely to come to a bad end—to say nothing of the individuals living under them—unless they learn to become at least as responsive to the basic needs of all their citizens as they are to the most insistent wants of the various articulate and influential interest groups and parties.

Most of Maslow's as well as Davies's discussion is highly speculative; only a beginning has been made. But their theory does lend itself to the production of testable hypotheses. For example, Almond's theory of political "input functions" (political socialization and recruitment; interest articulation; interest aggregation; political communication) and "output functions" (rule making; rule application; rule adjudication),[30] would seem to provide a fertile field for exploring what the participation in or other ego-involvement with each type of function can mean, in satisfying individual personality needs as well as wants. Moving in this direction we can perhaps get away from the customary clichés about the value of democracy, toward research-based knowledge on what (aspects of) democratic institutions have what kinds of value for human development.

I have argued elsewhere that the human goals of politics should be conceived in terms of maximizing individual freedom—psychological, social and potential.[31] Democracy and indeed every law and constitutional clause should be judged as a means to this end. A comprehensive treatment of norms of liberty with interrelationships and empirical consequences is necessary for this purpose, and so is a theory of human needs such as Maslow's, which in effect predicts that with increasing satisfaction of sustenance and security needs men's tendency will be to become less antisocial, more capable of respecting and eventually perhaps insisting on respect for the basic needs and liberties of others.

The normative research[32] to be recommended can be done

with far more precision than was attempted or achieved in the work on freedom just referred to. Perhaps philosophers working with political scientists can be expected to be active on this research frontier in future years. One good example of normative research of this kind, even though its reference to empirical data is for purposes of normative interpretation only, is Naess's study of Gandhi's ethics of conflict resolution.[33]

The burden of this paper, then, is to plead for an expansion and a more systematic articulation of the psychological and the normative perspectives of political behavior research. I propose as a normative basis the proposition that politics exists for the purpose of progressively removing the most stultifying obstacles to a free human development, with priority for the worst obstacles, whether they hit many or few—in other words, with priority for those individuals who are most severely oppressed; as Harrington points out with respect to the poverty stricken in the United States, they are also the least articulate, and the least likely to achieve redress by way of the ordinary democratic processes.[34] It is argued in this paper that the current preoccupation with pseudopolitical behavior carries conservative and anti-political implications, and that the best hope for a more politically useful reorientation of behavioral research—in addition to and beyond the comparative politics perspective—is to study how the various functions of government bear, and could bear, on the satisfaction of basic needs as well as conscious wants.

Among the questions to ask are these: What kinds of enduring satisfactions tend to be associated, for example, with particular participant and subject roles established by alternate forms of centralized or decentralized decision processes? Under what sociocultural and socioeconomic circumstances are majoritarian decision processes, of given types, likely to produce substantive satisfaction of the basic needs of, in Harrington's phrase, society's "rejects"?

As so often in our human condition, the dimensions of our ignorance appear to grow larger the closer we come to the most enduringly important issues of our social life. Much conceptual as well as basic psychological work remains to be done before our technical proficiency in the study of the relation of political forms to basic needs and to liberty can come to match the current work on analysis of voting patterns. But in this work political scientists should participate; our stakes in its progress are as high as anyone else's.

One particular type of research that should be pushed, as a much needed complement to the large supply of data on pseudopolitical behavior, is work that would focus on just how some citizens "graduate" from the role of pseudopolitical actor to that of political actor. Or, more accurately— for surely there are more pseudopolitical actors in the older age groups, "hardened in the school of life"—how it is that some categories of individuals (or individuals in some categories of situations) manage to remain concerned with ideals and with politics, i.e., with the welfare of their fellow men, all their lives?

A theory of human development is implied in the research approaches here recommended. It asserts that man is likely to become increasingly capable of being rational, or intellectual,[35] to the extent that he no longer needs the services of his beliefs and attitudes for the purpose of keeping his various anxieties in check. Deep-seated neurotic anxieties about one's worth as a human being predispose to right-wing or occasionally left-wing extremism, with glorification of ingroups or individuals, living or dead, along with hatreds against outgroups and deviants. Neurotic status anxieties predispose to eager adherence to whatever views appear expected in one's reference groups. Realistic fears about employment or future career prospects predispose against maintaining the luxury of political opinions at all, unless they are "safe." Only for individuals whose main anxiety problems have been faced and in some way resolved is it generally possible to think of and care about problems of politics in terms of standards of justice or the public interest, independently of personal worries.

The development of strictly political incentives in the individual, then, depends on a gradual process of liberation from a preoccupation with personal anxieties and worries. Stages in this process can be identified by research, although our concepts and instruments need some improvement before we can with confidence relate specific categories of political irrationality to (repressed or acknowledged) anxieties associated with specific levels in a hierarchy of human needs. Human nature being complex, so is the task of fully comprehending the dynamics of political behavior. My essential argument here is that we must face up to but not complacently accept, as the pseudopolitical outlook does, the fact that most of our citizens live too harassed lives or lack the education or opportunities for reflection to permit them the real satisfactions and the full dignity of democratic citizenship. We must pose the empirical problem of how the more stultifying pressures on adults and preadults can be reduced. A premature ruling out of the classic democratic citizenship ideal, with its stress on reason as a crucial factor in politics, would seem particularly inappropriate in our age of rapid technological change; never was the need for politics in the strict sense greater.

It is conceivable that our prospects for developing much larger proportions of political-minded citizens will improve substantially if or when the "cybernetics revolution" does away with our omnipresent worries about making a living.[36] On the other hand, unless educational and cultural resources can be expanded as rapidly, so that more people may be enabled to base their sense of identity and self-esteem on their own attributes or ideals rather than on their occupational roles, status anxieties and despair about lack of purpose in life might remain at present levels, and become aggravated for some. But the over-all prospects surely would be brighter, to the extent that more of the principal *real* worries on which our current anxieties feed were removed.

In any event, let us not as political scientists rule out the possibility that a real polity may emerge eventually—a community of people capable of giving some of their energies to political as distinct from pseudopolitical reflection and activity. A less utopian first step that may be hoped for is that many more political scientists will adopt a more political (or a less pseudopolitical) perspective in their theorizing and research. As the horizons of behavior research expand to encompass latent need-behavior as well as manifest want-behavior, our political science will not only produce a new order of intellectual challenge; it may also become a potent instrument for promoting political development in the service of human development.

REFERENCES

1. Alfred Cobban, "The Decline of Political Theory," *Political Science Quarterly,* 48 (1953), 335.
2. Heinz Eulau, *The Behavioral Persuasion in Politics* (New York: Random House, 1963), pp. 133–37.
3. Robert Dahl, *Modern Political Analysis* (Englewood Cliffs, N.J.: Prentice-Hall, 1963), p. 6.
4. "Priorities" here refers to norms for guiding the choice among conflicting needs and demands. Political ideals and visions of the good life enter in here, and would do so even if our knowledge of needs and of human nature were as extensive as our knowledge of demands and of social determinants of "public opinion."
5. Karl Mannheim employs a similar dichotomy of terms, though with different concepts, in his *Man and Society in an Age of Reconstruction* (New York: Harcourt, Brace & World, 1954), pp. 51–60.
6. Gabriel A. Almond, *The American People and Foreign Policy* (New York: Praeger, 1950), p. 4.
7. The term is from Leo Strauss. See his "Epilogue" in Herbert J. Storing, ed., *Essays on the Scientific Study of Politics* (New York: Holt, Rinehart & Winston, 1962), p. 326.

8. New York: Alfred A. Knopf, 1961.
9. Bernard R. Berelson, Paul F. Lazarsfeld and William N. McPhee, *Voting: A Study of Opinion Formation in a Presidential Campaign* (Chicago: University of Chicago Press, 1954).
10. Chicago: University of Chicago Press, 1956, p. 1.
11. This is not to deny that the Straussian position is more authoritarian and far less respectful of the right to radical dissent, as is to be expected when a corner on objective truth is being claimed. *Cf.* especially Leo Strauss, *What Is Political Philosophy, and Other Studies* (New York: The Free Press, 1959); and his "Epilogue" in Herbert J. Storing, ed., *op. cit.* See also Walter Berns, "The Behavioral Sciences and the Study of Political Things: The Case of Christian Bay's *The Structure of Freedom*," *American Political Science Review,* 55 (1961), 550–59.
12. Seymour Martin Lipset, *Political Man: The Social Base of Politics* (New York: Doubleday, 1960), esp. pp. 403 and 415.
13. An interesting attempt to evaluate the 1952 Presidential election in terms of five criteria of democratic consent (as opposed to nonrational responses to manipulated processes) is reported in Morris Janowitz and Dwaine Marvick, *Competitive Pressure and Democratic Consent* (Ann Arbor: Bureau of Government, University of Michigan, 1956). The five criteria are chosen somewhat haphazardly, but they are carefully and ingeniously operationalized and brought to bear on available data. The study shows what could just as well be done, in years to come, within a more carefully and systematically stated framework of political objectives and norms.
14. Though perhaps paradoxical, the statement is not self-contradictory. A democracy that guarantees many liberties to people of most persuasions, and in theory to everybody, may well be considered a liberal democracy. Freedom of speech and related freedoms have a strong appeal to most intellectuals, many of whom may become staunch conservatives *because* they believe in preserving their liberal democracy. Some, indeed, will become fixated on the need for defense of the social order to the point of ignoring the plight of poverty-stricken fellow-citizens whose formal liberty may seem worthless to themselves.
15. Ann Arbor: University of Michigan Press, 1962.
16. James M. Buchanan, "An Individualistic Theory of Political Process." Paper prepared for delivery at the 1963 Annual Meeting of the American Political Science Association, New York City.
17. Some of the milestones in this literature are Gabriel A. Almond, "Comparative Political Systems," *Journal of Politics,* 18 (1956), 391–409; Almond and James S. Coleman, eds., *The Politics of the Developing Areas* (Princeton: Princeton University Press, 1960); Almond and Sidney Verba, *The Civic Culture* (Princeton: Princeton University Press, 1963).
18. For contrast, consider this statement on the ways of other behavioralists: "The focus of the political behaviorist, however, does not seem to be a result of the state of political theory. Elections have been intensively studied because they lend themselves

to the methodology of empirical research into politics." Morris Janowitz, Deil Wright, and William Delany, *Public Administration and the Public—Perspectives Toward Government in a Metropolitan Community* (Ann Arbor: Bureau of Government, University of Michigan, 1958), p. 2.

19. *Cf.* Almond and Verba, *op. cit.,* and Lucian W. Pye, *Politics, Personality, and Nation Building: Burma's Search for Identity* (New Haven: Yale University Press, 1962).

20. Concepts of modernization or development are discussed by James S. Coleman in Almond and Coleman, eds., *op. cit.,* pp. 532–36; by Lucian W. Pye, ed., in *Communication and Political Development* (Princeton: Princeton University Press, 1963), pp. 14–20; and by Joseph La Palombara, ed., in *Bureaucracy and Political Development* (Princeton: Princeton University Press, 1963), chapts. 1 and 2.

21. *Political Man, op. cit.,* p. 115 and chapt. 4.

22. Fidel Castro's wide following in Latin America can be plausibly explained in these terms.

23. *Op. cit.,* p. 505 and chapt. 15.

24. *Ibid.,* pp. 440–41 and 478–79.

25. See especially Robert E. Ward and Dankwart A. Rustow, *The Political Modernization of Japan and Turkey* (Princeton: Princeton University Press, 1964).

26. However, we should not assume without inquiry that *all* pseudopolitical behavior is dysfunctional for all high-priority human wants and needs; not, of course, that all varieties of political behavior are to be preferred to pseudopolitical self-seeking or neurotic striving.

27. Joseph Tussman also stresses the danger of destroying the integrity of political communication when the modern bargaining approach to politics enters the "forum or tribunal" that a democratic electorate ought to constitute, according to classical theories of democracy. "We teach men to compete and bargain. Are we to be surprised, then, at the corruption of the tribunal into its marketplace parody?" *Obligation and the Body Politic* (New York: Oxford University Press, 1960), p. 109 and pp. 104–21.

28. Abraham H. Maslow, "A Theory of Human Motivation," *Psychological Review,* 50 (1943), 394 and 370–96. See also his *Motivation and Personality* (New York: Harper & Row, 1954).

29. *Human Nature in Politics* (New York: John Wiley, 1963), p. 28. Davies does not refer to La Palombara.

30. *Cf.* his introduction to Almond and Coleman, eds., *op. cit.*

31. *The Structure of Freedom* (Stanford: Stanford University Press, 1958; New York: Atheneum, 1965).

32. The term "normative research" may be puzzling to some, who think of research exclusively as systematically re(peated) search for empirical data, in the real world or in contrived experimental worlds. And "research" has been one of the empirical social scientist's proud banners in his uphill fight against the sometime supremacy of armchair speculators. In our time a less parochial use of "research" is called for, as a way of recognizing the close interplay between the empirical, normative and logical aspects of

inquiry that, as the present paper argues, is necessary for the further development of our knowledge of political as of other human behavior.

33. Arne Naess, "A Systematization of Gandhian Ethics of Conflict Resolution," *Journal of Conflict Resolution,* 2 (1958), 140–55; and Johan Galtung and Arne Naess, *Gandhis politiske etikk* (Oslo: Tanum, 1955).

34. Michael Harrington, *The Other America: Poverty in the United States* (New York: Macmillan, 1962; Baltimore: Penguin Books, 1963).

35. *Cf.* my "A Social Theory of Intellectual Development," in Nevitt Sanford, ed., *The American College* (New York: John Wiley, 1961), pp. 972–1005, esp. 978 and 1000–1005.

36. W. H. Ferry and 25 associates have recently issued a statement that received front-page attention in *The New York Times* and other newspapers. Under the title "The Triple Revolution: An Appraisal of the Major U.S. Crises and Proposals for Action" (Washington: Maurer, Fleischer, Zon and Associates, 1964), and referring to the revolutions in cybernetics, in weaponry, and in human rights, but particularly to the first of the three, Ferry *et al.* argue that there "is an urgent need for a fundamental change in the mechanisms employed to insure consumer rights" (p. 9), now that the problem of production has been solved and the problem of full employment has become impossible to solve with our present system. "We urge, therefore, that society, through its appropriate legal and governmental institutions, undertake an unqualified commitment to provide every individual and every family with an adequate income as a matter of right. This undertaking we consider to be essential to the emerging economic, social, and political order in this country" (p. 16).

6 : "Behavioristic" Tendencies in American Political Science

PETER H. MERKL

As Robert A. Dahl pointed out in 1961, the new school of the "behavioral approach" has come of age in the United States; a decade ago it was still a hotly debated issue. Its present status of "having arrived" may well mean that its original rationale no longer exists[1] (indeed, the origins of the behavioral movement are already being chronicled).[2] The present prestige of the behavioral school signifies by no means, however, the end of its opposition by a broad segment of American political scientists.

Opposition to the behavioral approach is especially voiced by groups of political scientists whose primary interest lies in political theory or public law, and by those who consider civic education the central purpose of political science. Their reactions, ranging from mild condescension to accusations of

This article is the author's adaptation of a more extended treatment, "Behavioristische Tendenzen in der Amerikanischen Politischen Wissenschaft," in *Politische Vierteljahresschrift*, 6 (March 1965), 58–86.

revolutionary or even subversive intent, tend to be offset, however, by the crusading zeal of certain behavioral scientists who are inclined to call the existing discipline of political science "unscientific" and "reactionary." Actually, the majority of research-minded American political scientists tend toward eclecticism. They spurn the behavioristic claim for an exclusive monopoly on scientific validity while sharing the behaviorists' concern for methodology, often using behavioral methods along with the conventional approaches as their judgment and the nature of the problem might suggest. Common sense is evidently the basic criterion of scientific validity underlying the eclectic approach.

Despite the decades of public controversy over the definition of "political behavior," there is still an astonishing amount of confusion about how to define it and how to distinguish the behavioral school from other approaches. This confusion stems in part from the differences of opinion among its proponents, not to mention its opponents, and in part from the inclination of successful revolutionaries to reinterpret history as their own antecedent, turning the important figures of earlier political science research into their precursors. This dialectical approach tends, of course, to dilute the definition.

One should furthermore point out the source of a misunderstanding to which the representatives of the behavioral school have addressed themselves only in the last few years: the distinction between "behaviorism" and the "behavioral approach." The original "behaviorism" was a school of psychology founded by James B. Watson and his colleagues that attempted to resolve the dispute about the content, structure, and processes of human consciousness by evading all questions about the content of the "little black box"—the soul, consciousness, subconsciousness; the subjective spirit; instincts, the nervous system. Instead, the science of psychology was said to be based simply on the relationship between the stimulus as it acts on the black box and the black box as it reacts to the stimulus.

Today, unlike the "black box psychologist" of the turn of the century, a representative of political behavioralism, such as Heinz Eulau, emphasizes that behavioralism does concern itself with the processes of cognition, feelings, and with evaluations of human consciousness.[3] This, however, does not clarify the essential character of the behavioral approach either: even the behavioristic psychologist has long since assumed certain contents to the black box. Eulau's argument is convincing only if we are prepared to assume that the criteria of a science of individual psychology and a science of politics are the same. But, in fact, the charge that the behavioral approach is "behavioristic" was never meant to indicate complete identification, and for this reason the parallelism cannot be automatically discarded. (At the very least one could claim that the behavioral approach resembles the present successors of the old behavioristic school of psychology far more than it does the American representatives of the "New Science of Politics," from Charles E. Merriam to Lasswell, whom the behavioral school often likes to claim as its precursors.) Although the emphasis of nonbehaviorists on purposive and rational capacity of political action does perhaps supply a more meaningful criterion for distinguishing between psychology and political science, most political situations and processes undoubtedly display as many important aspects of a behavioral nature as of purposive action. And it goes without saying that the behavioral aspects are more amenable to empirical research. To distinguish between behavior and action, therefore, does not imply a condemnation of the behavioral approach—provided the researcher merely intends to throw light on the political processes and does not intend to state that political man "behaves" and never "acts."

The problem is further complicated by the fact that Robert A. Dahl, David Easton, Heinz Eulau, and other prominent representatives of the behavioral school generally prefer to answer questions as to the character of the behavioral approach by saying what it is not. "Philosophical speculation, historiography, legal studies or moral considerations" are evidently not part of it.[4] Dahl typically speaks of a "behavioral mood," a mood critical of methods, a concern for methodology which lends to the behavioral approach a protest character. Unfortunately, both Dahl and Eulau define this critical mood so loosely and imprecisely that their formulations could be used almost as well to describe a number of modern political philosophers from Machiavelli to Marx and Freud; they too wanted to be more "realistic" than their precursors. Perhaps a more telling example of the typical ways of thinking of the behavioral school is Dahl's ingenious *A Preface to Democratic Theory*[5] in which various theories of democracy are cast in a form amenable to scientific logic and empirical verification. Eulau's path to the behavioral approach evidently began with similar thoughts about the empirical formulation of certain classical political theories. Eulau feels, in fact, that the behavioral school is the continuation of, and not just a critical reaction to, the classical school. A closer look at his definition of political behavior clears up the apparent contradiction. Eulau begins with a warning that conceptual definitions in such an old field of knowledge as politics will tend to bog down in words pregnant with symbolism, circular tautologies, or Thomistic essences, for these make an empirical or operational definition impossible. If you ask your students what politics is, you often receive the answer that it "has something to do with government, power, policy, influence, decision making, conflict," or even "authoritative allocation of values."[6] But if you ask what people do when they act in reference to these concepts, students often cannot give an answer. As Eulau suggests, such a question relating to religious life could be answered with praying, going to church, receiving communion, singing church songs, believing. In economics, it could be answered with producing, buying, selling, exchanging, investing, speculating, or consuming. Consequently political behavior, Eulau suggests, must be governing and obeying, persuading and mediating, promising and negotiating, forcing and representing, fighting and fearing. These activities and actions admittedly will not add up to a concept of the "political" in the conventional sense. However, they do supply an empirically viable basis and undoubtedly lie at the heart of political events. On the other hand, we have to take into account the subjective conceptual ideas of politics that the political actors themselves bring into their actions, and which they allow, in fact, to direct their activities.[7] Eulau sees no merit in the objection that his approach misses the "really important" problems of politics. The importance lies not in the nature of the question asked, but in the answer; it therefore cannot be anticipated without entanglement in metaphysical speculation.

How do other representatives and observers of the behavioral school characterize the behavioral approach to distinguish it from the more traditional schools? Evron M. Kirkpatrick names as a first characteristic the turning away from the once so popular institutional studies and their replacement by the exploration of the political behavior of individuals.[8] Dahl and Easton seem to agree. Eulau even sees institutions as systems of political behavior.

> Political institutions are behavior systems or systems of action. Just as they cannot exist apart from the persons whose behavior brings them into existence, so political behavior cannot exist apart from the network of interpersonal relations that we call political institutions.[9]

Instead of looking at the institutions themselves, such as the courts or, in other words, the fabric of legal decisions, the behavior-oriented political scientist explores judicial behavior, electoral behavior, legislative behavior, and administrative behavior as the objective regularities of political behavior within a given institutional frame. The stress on individual behavior also points to the psychological roots of the behavioral school, which go far back into the history of American political science,[10] but which even more are based on contemporary psychology.[11]

The second characteristic cited by Kirkpatrick is the attempt and desire to unite the study of political behavior with the similarly oriented disciplines of psychology, sociology, and anthropology. On this point Dahl, Easton, and also David B. Truman agree.[12] The movement to unify the social sciences is also a movement to make them more scientific, and to do so with the help of identical criteria and methods. Kirkpatrick's third characteristic of the behavioral approach is the concern for methodology and a search for more precise methods of observation, classification, and measurement, as well as stress on quantitative or statistical formulations wherever possible. As Easton has pointed out, this includes the systematic cataloguing of regularities of political behavior, the empirical verification of generalizations, and the self-conscious application of methods and quantification. The behavioral school is quite aware of the limitations of quantification in political research, but demands a strict separation of basic research and practical application in everyday politics as well as the separation of value judgments from value-free methods. A fourth characteristic, according to Kirkpatrick, is the development of systematic, empirical theories of political behavior, in particular in the form of empirically verifiable models—generally sets of related working hypotheses. Empirical theory is supposed to draw together individual research operations and give them purpose and significance within a larger structure, which in turn is to be united with the empirical theory of other social sciences.[13]

Beyond this framework, individual political scientists of the behavioral persuasion are free to develop their own specialties or their own plans for the fusion of traditional and novel methods of approach. Eulau, for example, distinguishes four main problems of behavioral research: (1) The identification of the units which are the object of research, such as individuals, small groups, communities, elites, mass movements, or whole nations; (2) The determination of the levels of analysis which cannot be limited by the conventional disciplinary boundaries without running the danger of reduc-

ing politics to psychological, economic, or cultural causation;
(3) The clarification of the relationship between empirical
theory and individual research operations, and (4) The
specification of the criteria used for the choice of methods.
On this basis Eulau builds up various theoretical models of
society. One such model is the social matrix of interpersonal
relations whose basic empirical unit is the individual role.
Public opinion research can explore the subjective role images
of citizens, judges, party functionaries, voters, etc., which
may lead to such enlightening studies as Eulau's study of
representatives in the state legislatures of American states.[14]
In this project the representatives were confronted with the
well-known role images of Edmund Burke and Rousseau, and
asked how they themselves visualized their roles as representatives. From the individual roles Eulau proceeds to the
"vertical groups" and inquires into the patterns of group
identification and loyalty of individuals as well as into the
influence of the groups upon their members. The vertical
dimension is followed by the horizontal dimension, the layers
of society which also lend themselves in many ways to empirical research.[15] A second theoretical system of explanation is
that of the "cultural framework" which includes the language,
thinking, and mores, the beliefs and the aesthetic sentiments
of a people, and can be broken down into subcultures of
groups or localities. For purposes of political research, it may
often be advisable to look for characteristic forms and images
of behavior in the macrocosm of the whole culture before
exploring the microcosm of individual behavior. Authoritarian behavior, for example, could be found just as well in
child rearing, in work situations or in the church as in macro-
politics. The competitive or gamesmanship character of
Anglo-American democracy may also be found in other areas
of life as well.

Eulau's version of the outline of behavioral research shows
that the approaches of the behavioral school often become
indistinguishable from the ways of thinking and the concepts

that conventional social science research has employed.[16] But one should always give him and other behaviorally-inclined political scientists credit for their honest effort to state their theoretical suppositions in the rigorously empirical and verifiable manner that many conventional political scientists, for reasons of their own, avoid. There can be no doubt that no true science of politics can be established without such intellectual honesty; and, while there may still be controversy about the exact definition and the limitations of the behavioral approach, there can be no doubt about its vitality. The astonishing and increasing number of research operations of recent date which apply the behavioral methods to the most varied fields of political science demonstrate its lively impetus.

The polemical literature about the behavioral approach is quite considerable, but generally throws more heat than light on the subject. A critical appraisal might bear the following aspects in mind, some of which have already been alluded to. First of all we have to assume that the so-callel political "sciences" in the United States and elsewhere were only to a limited degree intended ever to become scientific—in the sense of a natural science which examines frog legs under a microscope or reports the movement of the stars in the universe. There can be no doubt that many political scientists are as a matter of principle—and this to some degree applies even to the most "scientifically inclined"—personally involved in the sacred collectivity of their political community. They have dedicated their lives to making good citizens out of the young of the community and can, therefore, hardly be indifferent to the values and traditions of this community.[17] It is for this reason that some of them see in the quasi-natural science claims of the behavioral school a total ideology which threatens to dissolve the sacred bonds of the community: "The rise of the behavioral sciences could mean the disintegration of political science. For, first, it may mean that the social scientist, and more particularly, the Political Scientist, will cease to represent the public order which supports him."[18]

The exaggerated claims of some representatives of the behavioral school who threaten all aspects of the discipline with their revolution, regardless of the changing concepts and definitions of behavioral methods, tend to reinforce the sense of alarm of traditionally-oriented circles.

Secondly, our lives are taking place in the midst of a steadily accelerating process of social and technological modernization, the consequences of which have tended to threaten human relationships, existing communities, and the functionally optimal education and adjustment of working people in all phases of social life. This also applies to political scientists as a profession, undiminished by the fact that they may understand these processes theoretically. One should not be surprised by the sense of uneasiness with which the average political scientist must view the spread of new, more or less mathematical, methods in which he has not been trained, an attitude comparable to that of a skilled worker facing the automation of his special skill. The exalted position of university teaching gives the political science professor no more security against the inroads of the computers into the sacred realm of his specialty than other victims of technological or social progress possess. In fact, his well-trained intellect may tempt him to question elaborately the desirability and use of science or of progress itself.

Disregarding these ways of thinking, and reading the antagonists, pro and con, in the behavioral battle with the appropriate skepticism, it is not difficult to arrive at a balanced judgment. Such a judgment should be based first of all on a recognition of the limits of the application of behavioral methods—in so far as these methods can be clearly distinguished from non-behavioral methods. Primary value judgments and normative thinking[19] are beyond the pale of behavioral methods and play a role in general questions, such as whether democracy is good and authoritarian dictatorship bad, as well as in the content of questions and values that are fed into a computer program. These reservations also apply to the ideological overtones of the behavioral school. Secondly, such a judgment should be based on the recognition of the manifold contributions of the behavioral approach to empirical research, notwithstanding criticism of specific research operations. The behavioral school is undoubtedly right in its exhortation to be more conscious of method and more critical of the language of research. We need not entertain any illusions about the depth of wisdom that may be hidden underneath the inaccuracies and vagueness of the conventional usages of the language of politics. And, as a third point, the great merit of behavioral research in the building of theories should be recognized. The direct bearing of its models, theoretical systems, and computer programs on empirical research in politics appears to be the most valuable contribution of the behavioral school to the development of the whole discipline. Its benefits are likely to last long after the words "behavioristic" and "behavioral" school have been forgotten.

To put it a different way, empirical research in political science within the last decade has reached a level at which the development of empirical theory became absolutely necessary. The guardians of traditional political philosophy had long been entreated to assist with the formation of this empirical theory, but were evidently neither willing nor able to come to the aid of empirical research. It is true that this kind of theory has to be derived from induction rather than from Plato's Cave, although a healthy dose of the philosophy of science would not have been amiss.[20] At any rate, the formation of empirical theory was begun by the behavioral school and various political scientists who frequently are not even considered behavioral scientists. If the heretic intentions and exaggerated claims of the members of the behavioral school then came to open conflict with the "inquisition" of traditional political philosophy, this need not surprise anyone familiar with the strength of the sacred collectivity and the history of iconoclasm. The increasing undefinability of the limits of the behavioral school as compared to other new empirical methods already indicate the episodic character of the name "behavioral," which in fact was never accepted by some political scientists. Very soon, no doubt, new empiricists may regard the behavioristic pioneers of yesterday as narrow-minded traditionalists, while they in turn may anticipate a similar fate. But the resurgence of empirical theory and the flowering of empirical research that rests more heavily on "solid islands of theory"—the building blocks for the construction of a modern political science on a broad eclectic basis—are of lasting value.

REFERENCES

1. Robert A. Dahl, "The Behavioral Approach in Political Science: Epitaph for a Monument to a Successful Protest," *American Political Science Review,* 55 (December 1961), 763–72.
2. *Ibid.,* pp. 763–66; and David Easton, "The Current Meaning of 'Behavioralism' in Political Science," in J. C. Charlesworth, ed., *The Limits of Behavioralism in Political Science* (Philadelphia: American Academy of Political and Social Science, 1962), pp. 1–25.
3. Heinz Eulau, "Segments of Political Science Most Susceptible to Behavioristic Treatment," in Charlesworth, ed., *op. cit.,* pp. 30–31. See also Harold D. Lasswell and Abraham Kaplan, *Power and Society: A Framework for Political Inquiry* (New Haven: Yale University Press, 1950).
4. See Dahl, *op. cit.,* p. 763; and Heinz Eulau, *The Behavioral Persuasion in Politics* (New York: Random House, 1963), p. 7.
5. Robert A. Dahl, *A Preface to Democratic Theory* (Chicago: University of Chicago Press, 1956).
6. Eulau, *Behavioral Persuasion,* p. 4.
7. *Ibid.,* pp. 4–11, and sources cited there.
8. Evron M. Kirkpatrick, "The Impact of the Behavioral Approach on Traditional Political Science," in Austin Ranney, ed., *Essays on the Behavioral Study of Politics* (Urbana: University of Illinois Press, 1962), p. 12.
9. Eulau, *Behavioral Persuasion,* p. 16. See also Muzafer Sherif and Bertram L. Koslin, *The "Institutional" vs. "Behavioral" Controversy in Social Science with Special Reference to Political Science* (Norman, Oklahoma: Institute of Group Relations, 1960).
10. At least as far back as Graham Wallas' important *Human Nature*

in Politics (1908), and to Charles E. Merriam, *New Aspects of Politics* (1925).

11. See Charles E. Osgood's introduction to behavioristic psychology —the "missing link between biology and the social sciences"—in "Behavior Theory and the Social Sciences," in Roland Young, ed., *Approaches to the Study of Politics* (Evanston: Northwestern University Press, 1958), pp. 217–44.

12. See David B. Truman, "The Impact on Political Science of the Revolution in the Behavioral Sciences," in *Research Frontiers in Politics and Government* (Washington, D.C.: Brookings Institution, 1955), pp. 202–31; and David Easton, "Traditional and Behavioral Research in American Political Science," *Administrative Quarterly,* 2 (1957), 110–15.

13. See David Easton, *A Framework for Political Analysis* (Englewood Cliffs, N.J.: Prentice-Hall, 1965).

14. Heinz Eulau *et al.,* "The Role of the Representative: Some Empirical Observations on the Theory of Edmund Burke," *American Political Science Review,* 53 (September 1959), 742–56.

15. On this point, see also Heinz Eulau, *Class and Party in the Eisenhower Years* (New York: The Free Press, 1962); and Dwaine Marvick, ed., *Political Decision-Makers: Recruitment and Performance* (New York: The Free Press, 1961).

16. See Eulau, *Behavioral Persuasion,* chapts. 2 and 3. Also worth noting is the breadth of the concept of political behavior covered by selected readings in S. Sidney Ulmer, *Introductory Readings in Political Behavior* (Chicago: Rand McNally and Company, 1961).

17. See especially Russell Kirk, "Segments of Political Science not Amenable to Behavioristic Treatment," in Charlesworth, ed., *op. cit.,* pp. 49–67.

18. Francis G. Wilson, "The Behaviorist's Persuasion," *Modern Age,* 3 (1959), 316. This typical formulation not only denies science but also has a curiously relativistic ring.

19. On this point, see Mulford Q. Sibley, "The Limitations of Behavioralism," in Charlesworth, ed., *op. cit.,* pp. 68–93.

20. This absence of a sound foundation in the philosophy of science is often the weakest aspect of the new research methods. But now, see Abraham Kaplan, *The Conduct of Inquiry: Methodology for Behavioral Science* (San Francisco: Chandler Publishing Company, 1964); and Karl W. Deutsch, *The Nerves of Government: Models of Political Communication and Control* (New York: The Free Press, 1963), chapt. 1.

Index

Action, general theory of, 49, 58
Adorno, T. W., 83
Agger, Robert E., 7, 15*n*
Almond, Gabriel A., 11, 15*n*, 55, 70, 83, 126, 128, 133
American Business and Public Policy (Bauer, Pool, and Dexter), 15*n*
American Political Science Association, 4, 69-70, 75
American Political Science Review, 68*n*, 109*n*
American System, The (Grodzins), 15*n*
American Voter, The (Campbell et al.), 6, 81, 87-88
Analysis
  basic units of, 3
  convergence of institutional and behavior, 6
  of political development, 129-137
  synchronic versus diachronic, 6
  systemic and functional, 16-17

Anthropology, 39, 146
Appeals of Communism, The (Almond), 83
Aristotle, 13, 90, 112
Assumptions, 95-96
  normative, 14
Attitudes, analysis of, 43
Authoritarian behavior, 105, 147
Authoritarian Personality, The (Adorno et al.), 83

Bauer, Raymond A., 15*n*
Bay, Christian, 13, 109-140
  "Politics and Pseudopolitics," 13, 109-140
Beard, Charles A., 88
Behavior, study of individual or collective, 3
Behavioral approach, 68-92
  antipolitical orientation, 121-124
  bias toward liberal democracy, 121
  characteristics, 145-146
  Chicago school, 70

153

Behavioral approach (*cont'd*)
  controversies over, 3-21
  distinction between "behaviorism" and, 2, 142-143
  "Economic" approach, 17-18
  effect of World War II, 71
  future outlook, 85-90
  historical background, 69-80
  historical studies and, 87-89
  influence of European scholars, 70-71
  influence of foundations, 73-75
  "institutional" versus, 5-6
  limits of, 3
  literature on critical evaluation, 109-140
  models and methods, 8-9
  nature of, 76-80
  opposition to, 141-142
  present status, 141-152
  protest movement, 76-80, 144
  research, 73-75
  scientific outlook, 76, 80-84, 89-90
  sociological approach, 17-18
  value biases, 110
Behavioral sciences, 39-52
  definition, 39
  developments in, 39-52
    research techniques, 40-44
    theory, 44-50
  limitation on application of, 57-64
  revolution in, 38-67
Behavioral Sciences Program, 74-75
Behaviorists, 76
Bendix, Reinhard, 71
Benson, Lee, 88
Bentley, Arthur F., 50, 55
Berelson, Bernard, 74, 81, 118, 124, 128
Bergson, Henri, 96
Blau, Peter, 18
Bogardus, Emory Stephen, 43
Brogan, Denis William, 70
Bryce, James, 70
Buchanan, James M., 123-124
Buchanan, William, 6, 15*n*

Calculus of Consent, The (Buchanan and Tullock), 123-124

Campbell, Angus, 6, 15*n*, 81, 87
Cantril, Hadley, 83
Carnegie Foundation, 73
Catlin, G. E. G., 70
Center for Advanced Study in the Behavioral Sciences, 75
Change, patterns of, 27
"Chicago school" of political science, 50, 70
Citizens, political-minded, 135-137
Civic Culture, The (Almond and Verba), 15*n*, 128
Cohen, Hermann, 97
Coleman, James, 84
Colleges and universities, study of political science, 22-23
Commitment, 12
Communications, 49
  content analysis, 44
Communism, Conformity and Civil Liberties (Stouffer), 83
Communities, as systems of influence, 85
Comparative analysis of governments, 55, 124-129
Comte, Auguste, 28, 97-98
Concepts and definitions, 111-116
  political science, 29
Conformism, 11
Consensus, 87
Conservatism, 121
Content analysis, 44
Controversies in political science, 1-21
Converse, Philip E., 6, 15*n*, 81
Cross-sectional studies, 7
Cultures, study of, 106
"Cybernetics revolution," 136

Dahl, Robert A., 6-7, 15*n*, 56, 68-92, 124, 141, 143-144, 145-146
A Preface to Democratic Theory, 119-121, 128, 144
Data, collection and analysis of, 42
Davies, James C., 131-133
Decision-making, analysis of, 55-56
Democracy, 105
  needs and wants, 130-137
  normative theories, 117

political norms and, 116-121
Democratic theories, 116-121
Descartes, René, 103-104
Deutsch, Karl, 55, 85
Developing countries, 127, 132
Development, political, 124-129
Durkheim, Émile, 71

Easton, David, 4-5, 7, 22-36, 143, 146
Eclecticism, 142
"Economic" approach, 17-18
Einstein, Albert, 90
Eldersveld, Samuel J., 15n
Elections, see Voting behavior studies
Empirical political studies, 86-90
Encyclopedia of the Social Sciences, 40, 41
"Ethical neutrality," 11, 100
Eulau, Heinz, 1-21, 124, 143-148
"The Goal is Man," 110, 116, 129
European scholars, influence of, 70-71
Evolutionism, 98
Extremism, 135

Federal services, political scientists in, 23, 71
Fenno, Richard F., Jr., 15n
Ferguson, LeRoy C., 6, 15n
Ford Foundation, 74-75
Foreign policy, 55
Foundations, contributions to research, 73-75
Freedom, needed for scientific investigations, 12-13
Freud, Sigmund, 71

Galileo, 90
Gallup poll, 41
Gandhi, Mahatma, 134
Gaudet, Hazel, 74, 81
Gerth, Hans, 71
Goal formulation, 109-110
Goldrich, Daniel, 15n
Good and evil, 93-96, 98
Good society, 94, 108, 122
Grazia, Alfred de, 77
Grodzins, Morton, 4, 15n
Group dynamics, 44
    behavioral science theory, 46

small group studies, 47
"Group politics," 105
Guttman, Louis, 43

Hacker, Andrew, 109n
Harrington, Michael, 134
Heidegger, Martin, 96
Herring, E. Pendleton, 71-72
Historical studies, 6
Historical understanding, 106-107
Historicism, 106-108
Hobbes, Thomas, 90
Hoover Commission on the Organization of the Executive Branch of Government, 23
Hume, David, 112
Husserl, Edmund, 96
Hyman, Herbert H., 109n

Individuals
    attitudes and behavior of, 43
    behavioral science theory, 46
    development of political incentives, 135-136
    as empirical unit analysis, 17
Innovation, 2-3, 34
    in scientific development, 2, 4
    tension between tradition and, 8
Institutionalism versus behaviorism, 5-6
"Institutionalists," 51, 53, 64, 65
Institutions, 145-146
    behavioral science theory, 5-6, 44-47
    descriptions, 50-52
    emphasis on, 58-61
    research techniques, 50-54
    study of, 3
Intellectual conflicts, 1-3
"Intellectual treason," 110, 116
Interviews, 42-43
    conduct and analysis of, 57
    depth, 42
    techniques, 42-43
Involvement, 12

Kant, Immanuel, 103
Kent, Frank, 69
Kepler, Johannes, 90
Key, V. O., Jr., 15n, 70, 72, 117, 124
Kirkpatrick, Evron M., 145-146

Knowledge, quest for universal, 94-96

Labor unions, study of, 84-85
Lane, Robert E., 15*n*, 83
La Palombara, Joseph, 126-127, 132
Lasswell, Harold, 70, 75, 83, 143
Latin America, 128
Lazarsfeld, Paul, 43, 71, 74, 81, 118, 128
Leadership, 46-47, 53
Legislative committees, 63
Legislative System, The (Wahlke), 6, 15*n*
Legislatures, study of, 63, 147
Lenski, Gerhard, 18
Lewin, Kurt, 44
Lieber, Francis, 70
Likert, Rensis, 43
Lindblom, Charles E., 56
Lipset, Seymour Martin, 83, 84, 88, 121-122, 124, 127

McClosky, Herbert, 83
Machiavelli, 90
McPhee, William N., 118, 128
Mannheim, Karl, 48
Marx, Karl, 28, 71
Maslow, Abraham H., 131-133
Matthews, Donald R., 15*n*
Mayo, Elton, 44
Merkl, Peter H., 19, 141-152
Merriam, Charles E., 5, 50, 69-70, 75, 143
Methodenstreit, 4
Methodology, 32
  backwardness, 4-5
  behavioral approach, 81, 142, 144, 146
Methods in Social Science (Rice, ed.), 41
Michels, Robert, 71
Miller, Warren E., 6, 15*n*, 81
Models, 5
  creation and exploitation of, 49, 56
Moreno, J. L., 44
Mosca, Gaetano, 71
Murdoch, George P., 72

Naess, Arne, 134
Nationalism, 55

Needs and wants, 112, 125-126, 130-137
  evaluation of, 115-116
  priorities of needs, 131
  theoretical and conceptual task, 130
Negroes and the New Southern Politics (Matthews and Prothro), 15*n*
Neumann, Franz, 71
Neumann, Sigmund, 71
Newton, Sir Isaac, 90
Nihilism, 11, 98-99, 100
Nkrumah, Kwame, 132

Odegard, Peter, 75
Ogg, Frederic, 24
Opinion surveys, 42

Pareto, Vilfredo, 71
Parsons, Talcott, 48, 49, 58
People's Choice, The (Lazarsfeld, Berelson and Gaudet), 74, 81
Philistinism, 11
Philosophy, 94-95; *see also* Political philosophy
Plato, 13, 14, 18, 100, 112, 130
Policies, studying ultimate end of, 116
Political Behavior (Kent), 69
Political Behavior: Studies in Election Statistics (Tingsten), 69, 73
Political Ideology (Lane), 15*n*
Political Man (Lipset), 83
Political Parties: A Behavioral Analysis (Eldersveld), 15*n*
Political philosophy, 4, 86, 93-108
  assumptions, 95-96
  political science and, 9-10
  problems of, 96-108
  rejection of, 96-97
Political science
  "behavioristic" tendencies, 141-152
  condition of, 22-36
  goal formulations, 109-110
  impact of behavioral sciences on, 38-67, 141-152
  new tendencies, 52-57
  political philosophy and, 9-10

public policy and, 5
training in, 23, 75
Political scientists, 148-149
responsibilities, 2, 5, 114-115
training, 23, 75
Political System, The (Easton), 22n
Politics
analysis of political systems, 84
concept of, 111-112
definition, 13
pseudopolitics and, 109-140
tradition and innovation, 1-21
Population sampling, 40-41
Positivism, 10-11, 16, 97-98, 101
historicism versus, 106-108
weaknesses, 101-108
Power, locus of, 25-27, 35
Power of the Purse, The (Fenno), 15n
Preface to Democratic Theory, A (Dahl), 119-121, 128, 144
President's Committee on Administrative Management, 23
PROD (journal), 77
Propaganda, 132
Prothro, James W., 15n
Pseudopolitics
behavior, 124-129
definition, 112-113
outlook, 135-136
Psychological phenomena, 129
Psychology, 39, 149
behavioristic school, 142-143
Public Opinion and American Democracy (Key), 15n, 117
Public opinion research, 117-118, 147
Public policy and political science, 5

Research Frontiers in Politics and Government (Truman), 38n
Research in political science, 14
basic and applied, 59
in behavioral sciences, 14-15, 40-44
case studies, 61
concepts, 29-31
conventional, 50-52

distribution of social power, 25
emphasis on institutions, 58-61
empirical, 4-5, 15, 86-90
group dynamics, 44
insights, 28-30
limitations of quantification, 146
methodology, 32
misuse of materials, 62-64
new tendencies, 52-57
normative, 133-137
panel techniques, 43
political significance, 114-115
present state, 22-36
problems of, 22-36, 146-147
projecting trends, 28
sample survey techniques, 40-44
technique for controlled observations, 33
techniques unrelated to, 61-62
terminology, 29, 31
Role, concept of, 49
Rulers and the Ruler, The (Agger), 7, 15n

Sample-survey method, *see* Survey methods
Scientific methods, 104-106
behavioral approach and, 76, 80-84, 89-90
of collecting evidence, 15
Sears, Robert, 62
Shils, Edward A., 49, 58
Simon, Herbert, 18, 47, 49, 70
Snyder, Richard C., 49, 55-56
Social power, 25
Social Science Research Council (SSRC), 71-72
Committee on Political Behavior, 72-73, 75, 77, 78
Social sciences, 146
behavioral sciences, 39
function of, 99
scientific development in, 7-8
tension between tradition and innovation, 8
Society, definition, 103
"Sociological" approach, 17-18
Sociology, 39, 71, 146
political science and, 3, 71

Socrates, 18, 19, 90, 100
Speculation, 90
Speier, Hans, 71
Stokes, Donald E., 6, 15*n*, 81
Stouffer, Samuel A., 83
Strauss, Leo, 9-11, 13, 93-108, 121
  attack on behavioralism, 9
  school of, 4, 18-19
  "What is Political Philosophy?" 9
Study of politics, 22-36
  ancient and modern ways, 1-21
  basic units of analysis, 3
  behavioral and historical methods, 6-7
  in colleges and universities, 22-23
  controversies, 1-21
  core and periphery of, 18-19
  cross-sectional, 7
  place of value in, 3
Survey methods, 6, 40-44, 73
  analysis of attitudes, 43
  questions and questionnaires, 42
  techniques, 40-44
Swanson, Bert E., 15*n*

Theories of political behavior, 146
  antiquarianism, 4-5
  behavioral sciences, 44-50
  empirical, 146-147
Thurstone scale, 43
Tingsten, Herbert, 69, 73
Tocqueville, Alexis de, 90
Toward a General Theory of Action (Parsons and Shils, eds.), 49, 58
Tradition, 2-3

  in scientific development, 2-3
  tension between innovation and, 8
Trow, Martin, 84
Truman, David B., 5, 38-67, 70, 73, 78, 146
  "The Implications of Political Behavior Research," 78-80
Tullock, Gordon, 123-124

Union Democracy (Lipset, Trow, and Coleman), 84
"Universalistic scheme," 13-14
University of Chicago, 5
University of Michigan, 72, 75
  Survey Research Center, 73, 74
Utilitarianism, 98

Value judgment, 9-12, 79, 98-103, 149
  moral problems and, 11-13
  problems of, 101-108
  rejection of, 103-104
  value conflicts, 3, 103-104
Van Dyke, Vernon, 77
Verba, Sidney, 15*n*, 109*n*, 128
Voting: A Study of Opinion Formation in a Presidential Campaign (Berelson, Lazarsfeld, and McPhee), 118, 128
Voting behavior studies, 48, 73-74, 81-82, 88, 118
  analysis of, 6, 55, 118, 128

Wahlke, John C., 6, 15*n*
Wallas, Graham, 50
Watson, James B., 142
Weber, Max, 48, 70, 71, 103
Whitehead, Alfred North, 96
Who Governs? (Dahl), 6, 15*n*